A LIFE LIVED MEDIUM

A LIFE LIVED MEDIUM

A PSYCHIC'S JOURNEY FROM
FEARFUL TO *ALMOST* FEARLESS

Jennifer Bierma

Wise Ink Creative Publishing

A LIFE LIVED MEDIUM © copyright 2019 by Jennifer Bierma. All rights reserved. No part of this book may be reproduced in any form whatsoever, by photography or xerography or by any other means, by broadcast or transmission, by translation into any kind of language, nor by recording electronically or otherwise, without permission in writing from the author, except by a reviewer, who may quote brief passages in critical articles or reviews.

ISBN 13: 978-1-63489-206-3

Printed in the United States of America
First Printing: 2019
23 22 21 20 19   5 4 3 2 1

Cover design by Emily Mahon
Interior design by Patrick Maloney

Wise Ink Creative Publishing replaces every tree used in printing their books by planting thousands of trees every year in reforestation programs. Learn more at wiseink.com.

This book is dedicated to my Gramma, Shirley, who crossed over to the other side only a few months ago. Her love of the tilt-a-whirl, good books, and unexpectedly humorous comments impacted me in a way that I cannot give words to. I can only wish that my book graces the library on the other side and fills her with pride. The loss of a loved one can be a profound call to action in life, and this book was inspired by the loss of many.

INTRODUCTION

So many psychics, mediums, and healers live their lives just under the radar for fear of dealing with skeptics, looking like a fraud, and overall, being judged. So many do not give themselves the permission or the opportunity to "live large": they settle instead for a life lived medium. They are known by family, friends, and clients as amazing healers, amazing seers, amazing fill-in-the-blank, but to the world they are something much milder, something tamer and more middle of the road. They are virtually unknown because they are afraid to find their voices in a judgmental world.

It is time that we stop. It is time that we step out of our secluded, medium-sized lives, find our voices, and live a large life in our medium world.

My life has been far from tame. My experiences have made me successful in business, a leader in life, strong-willed and vibrant. Rather than denying the experiences that helped to shape those qualities in my life, I want to embrace them and help others to see that in a world full of XL drinks and XS clothing, sometimes being a Medium has its perks.

My story may not be your story in the details, but I would guess that my story is your story at heart. I am allowing myself to be vulnerable in this moment. Like most of us, I have life experiences that may not be perceived in the best light. But I am allowing myself to be fully human so I can tell my story as only I can.

I saw it in a dream, or I suppose you could call it a vision. A beautiful, blond-haired, blue-eyed boy, about five or six years old, stood over my bed, fighting back tears as he told me how sad he was that he hadn't been born yet.

"When do I get to come see you again?"

He was right there; he was always right there. I reached out to touch him on the cheek. I could hear the emotion in his voice. He was distraught, and I was worried about him. In this moment, he felt much more human than ever before. I felt the tug of the blanket as he tried to wake me up, the texture of his soft skin as he touched my hand, and his breath on my cheek as he whispered in my ear.

I was twenty-two at the time, and he had been with me as long as I could remember. When I was a child, I didn't understand his presence. He was comforting at times but scary at others. He would appear out of nowhere in my dark room and stand over my bed. He would get angry and yell at me when I didn't listen or I didn't understand something he said. Other times, he would linger in the background to give me a giant smile of support when I was in trouble or pushing through my comfort zone to try something new. His presence was confusing to me.

With each year, our bond solidified more. Although he never aged, we grew up together. He was my best friend. But now, this vision was far different from the visions I'd had when I was young. It was the most heartfelt interaction I'd ever had with him. It is a vision that I will never forget.

I don't know who I'm kidding, calling him a vision. I am a medium: always have been and, more than likely, always will be. I have seen things that others can't see for as far back as I can remember. Spirits, angels, guides, ghosts, demons, and other light beings have been showing up in my life since I was two years old, maybe earlier.

That little boy, William, is a very real part of my life, but I don't always tell people about him, even though I fondly call my communication style "blurting." I hide this part of my life not because I am ashamed of him, but rather because there are still days when I struggle with the societal labels of *crazy, mentally ill,* or *weird*. I worry that I have some imbalance that makes me see things that aren't really there. I fear what others think about me. Those worries and fears are things that I have continually fought to overcome. Even after thirty-six years and a whole lot of right answers, some days I just have to trust my visions and deliver the messages that are brought to me. "Crazy" or not.

In recent years, I have started to receive channeled messages: weird writings using words that I wouldn't normally use, talking about things that I have no reason to know about. Those days are immensely draining and extremely confusing. I can't get my bearings and often have no clue what I am writing until I go back to read it later. Some days, I pray that I won't get those messages anymore. Some days, I pray that the messages will make more sense. More often, I pray that the messages will prove that what I am seeing and hearing is real.

I have had experiences of clairvoyance, clairsentience, clairaudience, and clairolfaction (clairalience). All that means is that I see, feel, hear, and smell the paranormal. The funny thing is, after all these years, I still have a hard time saying that I have mastered any of these traits. In fact, my worst nightmare is when a skeptic steps forward to grill me about their grandmother who passed away twenty years ago. At those moments I feel like my gift is a curse. Success isn't guaranteed: sometimes I don't trust myself and fail miserably, and sometimes a spirit decides not to participate.

In those moments I feel like I am back in grade school on test day. I am sure you know the feeling. You are sitting at your desk, looking at the multiple-choice questions (or, as we called it, multiple guess). You *know* the right answer, but at the last minute you second-guess yourself and change it. When you get the test back, you say, "I knew I was right. Why did I change my answer?!" Well, my life is a lot like that. Yours probably has its moments too: "Why didn't I say that part out loud? Why did I wait to tell her that until she told me XYZ?" Why? *Why? WHY?* A barrage of second-guessing followed by a whole lot of self-doubt.

For years, I have been called to tell my story and dragged my feet. It wasn't until recently that I realized that my story is meant to help others heal. It is meant to help people see that their gift to this world is being who they truly are, regardless of what the world deems normal. It is meant to help people walk through the fear of being themselves and their fears about what society thinks they should be.

I grew up with this self-inflicted notion that because I didn't like to read, I wasn't allowed to be an author. I felt that I wasn't allowed to use one of my gifts because my best friend was an avid reader and wrote all the time, my grandmother was a librarian, my mom loved to read, and my sister did too. It wouldn't be fair if I wrote a book before one of them did. They had put in their time with all that reading, and I thought they needed to be rewarded. I felt like I didn't deserve to have a book because I hadn't put in that time. But I am done waiting. It is my turn.

The human brain is a funny thing and likes to play tricks on us. Therefore, some of my facts may be skewed by my five-year-old mind or my aging thirty-six-year-old one, and some of the dialogue with spirits may be paraphrased or summarized. Either way, I will tell my story as I remember it. To be respectful of the privacy of friends, family, and acquaintances, many of the names in my book have been altered.

You will notice that in sections of this book, I will use the words *ghost* and *spirit* interchangeably, even though I now know that there is a distinct difference between the two. Ghosts are unintelligent projections of energies that are stagnant in a space. They cannot answer specific questions and they continually repeat movements, scenes, or phrases. They are like a movie stuck on repeat. Spirits are intelligent beings. They interact with other beings as if they were still on this earth in human form. They make decisions, hold conversations, and oftentimes can move physical items to get their point across. I use the words "ghost" and "spirit" interchangeably to help you see the confusion and fear that I faced as a child who knew nothing about the paranormal world . . . or rather, didn't know that I knew anything about it.

All that I ask is that you read my story with an open mind and realize that we are not so different. We all have experiences that make us feel "crazy" or "weird." We all have our own perception of what normal is or isn't, and we all deserve to have our story heard so that we can help to empower others to raise their voices. My hope is that my story helps at least one person understand that their normal is not the normal of everyone else, and that it is okay to be different.

If you are unfamiliar with a paranormal term used in these pages, please check the glossary in the back of the book. I have also included sporadic Messages of Clarity with questions for you to ponder and tips to help you with your own gifts or those of your loved ones. I hope they will give you the opportunity to ingest the information in the book in a freer and less structured way. If it feels right for you, please take time to read those sections and do some journaling on how the stories have affected you or what questions they have brought up for you. Such questions are often a calling from your guides to dig deeper into your own gifts. Do it! You won't be disappointed by what you learn about yourself and others!

1

EYES OF THE DARK

*Hope is being able to see that there is light
despite all of the darkness.*
—Desmond Tutu

As a child, I would lie in bed at night and try to figure out ways to get my parents to come to my room. Nighttime was my live-action nightmare. Parades of strangers walked through my room, telling me stories that were often far too graphic for a child. As an empath, I could feel their fear, sadness, and pain as they shared their stories. As they spoke, I could feel their wounds. I heard the raw hurt in their voices and cowered at their anger when I didn't know how to help them. They would shake me awake, pull at my covers, and yell to get my attention. How could anyone understand that as a child?

There were moments when my fear was so great that I just wanted it to go away. *I* wanted to go away. I hid in my closet and hoped that if I curled up under my blanket I would suffocate. I was young and didn't realize that a crocheted blanket with holes in it breathes—thank goodness. Ironically, I thought that death would stop the dead people from talking to me.

When my suffocation attempts failed, I convinced myself that if my parents came to my room, the strangers standing over my bed would go away. Everything would be "normal." Of course, it never worked for more than a brief moment because this *was* my normal. The strangers just stepped aside until my parents walked out of the room . . . but I kept trying.

One particular night, when I was seven, William was in my room again, digging through the backpack hanging behind my door. I was terrified. I had told my parents that he did this often. Without questioning it, my parents would comfort me with hugs and reassure me that it was okay before leaving. They always left the door open a crack so I had extra light in the room.

By this point, I was starting to believe I was "too old" to be scared at night. So, to get my parents to come to my room, I had to pretend that I was hurt. I lay in my cozy bed, knowing that if I cried my parents would come running to save their baby girl. They were sound asleep in their bedroom across the hall, so I would need to cry louder than I had ever cried before to get their attention. The problem was, I couldn't cry on command: I would really have to hurt myself. My forethought may have been lacking at that age, but my problem-solving skills and persistence were off the charts.

My twin bed had a curved, light cherry wood frame, a short headboard, and a footboard to match. Multicolored flowers and cream diamonds showered my sheets across a yellowed cream background. I clung to those sheets as if they were a miniature barricade to protect me from the people around me.

I plotted the scenario out in my head. If I hit my head hard enough on the headboard I would have no choice but to cry. So began Operation Cry Like You Mean It. I hit my head once. It wasn't hard enough; it just created a dull ache across the back of my head and made me anxious about the next try. I looked around the room and saw William standing there, looking at me in disbelief. Twice: my head felt like someone had clocked me with an old work boot. William's eyes widened, and he said gently, "Why are you doing that?" *Third time's the charm*—it had to be because there was no going back now. I hit the back of my head so hard that I reached up, expecting to feel the dampness of warm blood dripping down my skull. There was none. The only dampness was the stream of tears that fell from my eyes and landed on my pillow. Pain and fear combined, creating a river of tears and waves of sobs that soon became uncontrollable. I felt terrible and hopeful at the same time. The sobs brought my mom more quickly than I expected.

"Fejner, what's wrong?" my mom asked, using my nickname to help soften the words. My reply was simple: "I . . . (sob, sob) . . . hit . . . my . . . (sob, sob, sniffle) . . . my . . . head." There was no discussion of my fear or just how I hit my head, just a few long hugs and the usual reassuring "It'll be okay" until I had calmed down. Eventually my mom went back to her warm, safe bed, and I went back to my dark room and the fear.

For a long time, I thought I was scared because it was dark at night. I always heard people talk about being afraid of the dark. As hard as I tried to convince myself that I was like everyone else and afraid of the dark itself, I knew that it wasn't true. I wasn't very convincing, not even when I was just trying to convince myself. I knew that I was afraid of the people in my room. I remember telling my friends, at the age of eight, "I am not afraid of the dark, I am afraid of what is in the dark." The statement confused and terrified my friends more than I could have imagined. They didn't want to believe me, but at the same time, they were afraid to come to my house. Mostly because I told them what was in the dark. Well, my dark, anyway.

There was nothing too scary in the darkness of my room: just William, a man with long hair that William called Jay, and, most of the time, a lot of other people at once. All of them standing around, telling me things that I didn't quite understand as a five-year-old . . . a six-year-old . . . a seven-year-old . . . . Dang, sometimes I don't even understand now!

They weren't scary people; they were just like you and me . . . only dead. Some lived in my house, and others just popped in to ask for help when they needed it. They talked to me as if I knew them, and at times it was as if they were long-lost family members sharing our history. This familiarity just created more fear for me. I had no idea who these people were, and yet they shared everything with me. Fear was so constant for me that a small portion of my seven-year-old psyche was becoming numb to it. Fear, for me, was starting to morph into some other emotion that I couldn't explain.

Still, part of me felt comforted by the trust that these strangers placed in me. I started to form a sense of responsibility for them and everyone else around. Even though I was scared of these strangers in my room, I started to believe it was my job to care for them.

However, the intensity of their emotions was burdensome for a child. Their emotions were far more profound than what most children experience at this age, and I started to take that weight onto my own shoulders. I internalized their pain, their sadness, and their anger and held onto them as if they were my own.

I wondered why my family didn't acknowledge the other people in our house or talk to them. It intensified my sense of responsibility but at the same time created a sense of seclusion. I started to feel very alone.

My parents never told me that I had an overactive imagination or that there was no little boy behind my door at night. I never had reason to doubt what I was seeing. My morphing fear and sense of responsibility were completely justified and normal in my young subconscious. My parents always told me everything would be okay. Even fraught with emotion, I believed them, and I am grateful for that.

Back then, I was far more scared of William than anyone else. His constant chatter seemed extremely personal to me. It was as if he knew my family. He knew everything about me: what I liked to eat, the songs I sang in the shower, every fear I ever had. Most of all, he knew how to push my buttons. He was a weird part of my family, the scary little brother I never had in the physical world. He was *always* around, and no one else talked about him. I loved him, hated him, and feared him all at the same time.

He tortured me with his presence like any normal little brother would. Every night I would lie awake and stare at the door to my bedroom as he dug through my backpack. He took my homework, my books, my show-and-tell, and hid them so that I would forget to bring them to school in the morning. I almost always forgot to look in my backpack before I left. Then he tagged along to school just so he could laugh at me when I couldn't find my stuff. Eventually, I started to remember to check my bag before I left, and thank goodness: explaining why I didn't have my homework was very hard when my excuse was that the little boy behind my door took it. My teachers would just look at me. I don't think they ever talked to my parents about my excuse. Either that, or my parents had some very strange conferences but never talked to me about them.

It was William's routine to join us for dinner and make faces at me. I was constantly in trouble at the dinner table for laughing too much, partly because of William and partly because of my sister. Sometimes I would get sent to my room for being disruptive at the table. Then I would lie in my doorway and repeatedly ask, "Can I come out now? Can I come out now?" I didn't want to be in my room alone, day or night. It was like Grand Central Station, heaven and hell edition, in there.

William's favorite pastime was playing tricks on me, and I was not thrilled about it. The worst involved standing outside the shower while I was in there. He would push the shower curtain against my skin so that it would get stuck to me. It was creepy. Showers were already an issue for me; add William into the mix and I was more terrified there than in my bed at night.

Our relationship was hard for me to understand as I grew up. Something inside me said that I wasn't supposed to talk to him, like he was a stranger, and yet another part of me trusted him implicitly. Despite that confusion, I learned from him. He taught me that ghosts and spirits had been human at one time. Sometimes they need attention or love, or just to be heard. Most of all, like the living, they still have a sense of humor! We might find it creepy at times, but they need to find a way to stay amused for all eternity. Most of us only have to worry about amusing ourselves from minute to minute.

MESSAGES OF CLARITY

My childhood character and emotional responses were formed from my experiences, others' reactions to them, and my own creative ways of coping with them. People ask me all the time how parents with intuitive children should respond to their kids, and I always tell them that I don't know if there is a right answer. I do know there are ways that you can talk to your children (or anyone who shows signs of intuitive sensitivities) to show them they are not being judged and that they are loved and supported.

If a loved one begins talking to you about seeing or feeling unusual things or having fears about certain events, times of the day, or activities that seem abnormal to you, here are a few suggestions for judgment-free communication.

1. Explain that you would like to understand more about how they are feeling or what they are seeing. This shows them that you are coming from a place of curiosity rather than judgment.

2. Ask them to describe how they feel when different energies, beings, or sensations are being experienced. Also ask them if there is a certain time of the day or situation when they feel these experiences are occurring.

3. If they are fearful of someone they see or feel, explain to them that they have the power to tell the being to go away.

4. Teach them to ask the angels, their spirit guides, or loved

ones who have already passed away to give them protection or sit with them when they are scared.

5. Assist them in picking out healing stones or crystals to help them feel safe and protected. Giving them permission to pick out healing stones or crystals based on what feels good to them will allow them to develop a sense of what helps with their specific needs. We are all energetically in tune with the items that will assist us in our own healing.

6. If you are picking out stones or crystals for other people to assist in protection and safety, ask your spirit guides to assist you. There are also many healing stones and crystals that are generally associated with protection, such as black tourmaline, smoky quartz, amethyst, labradorite, and obsidian.

7. Last, but not least, work on your own fears about spirits, ghosts, demons, and so on. If you are clear about your own beliefs and fears, your children and the people around you will follow your lead. When we get our own emotions under control, it is easier for those around us to feel safe enough to share their fears, worries, and emotions.

2

OUIJA RATHER?

Ask, and it shall be given you; seek, and you shall find; knock, and it shall be opened unto you.
—Matthew 7:7 (KJV)

Like many children, my sister Jessi and I used to play with the Ouija board. It was our go-to pastime after school, the exciting "new" thing . . . or, rather, the old thing that came back over and over again, tricking kids into thinking it was a game. Unfortunately, Ouija boards are not a game and often open up a source of energy that most people don't understand or have the means to control. Ouija boards are a divining tool—I truly understand that, now that I'm older. They connect universal energy, or the energy of those who have passed away, to our living energetic frequency. In other words, it is like a phone call between the dead and the living.

Most of the kids in my elementary school class didn't believe in the Ouija board. Many of them thought that the other kids were pushing the planchette, or indicator, as we called it, around the board to spell out the things they wanted the other kids to see. That was true a lot of the time, but not in my house. I knew, and I am pretty sure my sister knew, we were truly talking to people who had passed away. I knew because we talked to William often. Even though I didn't need the Ouija board to talk to him, sometimes it was fun to pretend like I did. As I realized that other kids couldn't see the people we were talking to, the inkling in the back of my mind that I was not "normal" started to grow into a knowing.

It was fun to be normal and do things the other kids were doing. Still, I was always accused of pushing the indicator because I always knew what the spirit was saying before anyone else. When we talked to William, he fumbled through the alphabet, trying to spell the words out loud to himself. He was still young, not the greatest at spelling, and he made mistakes often. Sometimes he would ask me how to spell a word, and when I didn't respond, he would get upset with me. "Why won't you help me? Why are you being so mean?" he'd say, and with that, he would leave. Midsentence. The other kids were left wondering where the "ghost" went. I didn't want the other kids to know I was talking to him, so I would sit there, heartbroken that William was so upset with me, while I tried to fit in with my peers. "Where would a ghost have to go?" I'd ask. "Maybe he just didn't want to talk to us anymore."

In fourth grade I realized that I could communicate with the ghosts nonverbally. My own irritated internal monologue—the statements you never want anyone to hear—tipped me off. That day, William was pressing my buttons: "You never listen to me!" he accused. "You don't play with me!" At that time, it felt like he was *always* in my space, giving me no choice but to pay attention to him; I rolled my eyes and thought, *If you would leave me alone, I might want to!* I was shocked when his eyes turned sad and his tiny voice quavered, "You don't like me anymore?" I thought, *Did I say that out loud? No, I didn't! Can he hear what I'm thinking?*

He looked up at me and answered, "Yeah." Then he slunk back down next to me and bowed his head.

"Wait! You can hear what I think?" He kept staring at the ground. I wasn't sure whether he was sad about my mean comment or ashamed that he hadn't told me sooner. Indignant, I yelled, "Why didn't you tell me?"

He looked up at me, shrugged, and said, "I didn't know." This whole time, he'd thought I knew that he could hear my thoughts.

This conversation started my unofficial training on intentional communication with spirits. Their assumption seems to be, "If you don't want me to listen, you have to say so." It sounds so simple, but with the number of spirits around me, who did I tell not to listen? Should I just start my day by yelling out, "Stop listening to me!"? I had so many questions, and over the next year my conversations with William answered many of them. I learned that I could allow spirits to hear only the thoughts I wanted them to.

While it made hiding my gifts easier, it also made me feel like a target for that "crazy" label. When I heard people talk about "hearing voices," I would panic. Between the angels, spirits, spirit guides, and my own thoughts, I hear voices in my head all the time. As I grew older, I struggled to discern what would classify me as crazy. *If I talk to dead people, does that make me crazy? If I mentally talk to myself, does that make me crazy?* I started to fear that people could read my mind just like the spirits could and that I would be found out.

Each time we pulled out the Ouija board I feared that someone would hear my conversations as we watched the indicator move around the board. The Ouija board fueled my anxieties in other ways, too. Jessi figured out that she could use it to scare me—just like any older sister would do to younger siblings. One day she was downstairs with her friend Mary and the Ouija board. I was upstairs in the bathroom. As I sat down on the toilet, the shower curtain started thrashing around violently. It was like a cat had gotten wrapped in it and was trying desperately to get out. But there was no cat; I was in the bathroom, all by myself. I screamed bloody murder and just about peed on the floor as I ran to the other side of our small bathroom.

I could hear Jessi's footsteps pounding as she and Mary ran up the basement stairs. They were laughing so hard they couldn't catch their breath, gasping for air and then laughing harder.

"What's . . . hahahahaha . . . wrong?" Jessi finally cackled through the bathroom door. I was pulling my pants up, almost in tears, trying to sort out what had just happened so that I could tell my big sister.

"I was sitting on the toilet and the shower curtain started moving on its own!" Foolishly, I thought she would be sympathetic to my fear. I heard a pause and more laughter. I flung the door open and demanded, *"What is so funny?* It was scary!" She laughed even harder, grabbing her obviously cramping stomach.

Finally, she gasped, "We were playing the Ouija board and told William to scare you if he was really here! I guess he's here!" More laughter.

I was angry. Really, really angry. I didn't think it was a funny joke at all. I was already scared to be alone in our house, I already saw people everywhere, and now they were having spirits sneak-attack me in the bathroom!

I stormed past them, went into my room, and slammed the door. That night, I couldn't sleep. I was scared that someone would sneak up on me and scare me. I could deal with spirits when I could see them coming, but when they didn't show themselves, it was a whole different ball game. From that point on, I didn't want anyone to know that I got scared. It changed the way that I dealt with my emotions and how I expressed them to the world. I started to change the way that I interacted with my own feelings. If I felt fear, I would morph it into a different emotion or sensation altogether. I taught myself to control my external expression of fear. I started to hit the internal mute button and walk away from it. In my head, and only in my head, I became fearless.

3

STIRRING IT UP

In the choice between changing one's mind and proving there's no need to do so, most people get busy on the proof.
— John Kenneth Galbraith

After the shower-curtain incident, I started questioning how often spirits were around me when I didn't see them. Up until that point, I thought I could see them all the time. I didn't realize it was far more complicated than that or that I could turn off that part of my brain and block what I was seeing. I also didn't realize that the spirits could make themselves be seen or unseen. That led to even more questions and started a chain reaction of spiritual growth. I started to test the spirits. I began asking them to do things to show that they were there. What my young brain didn't realize was that if they didn't *want* to do it, they wouldn't do it. My tests weren't very scientific, and many of the spirits didn't respond too kindly to being tested. Being told what to do by a nine-year-old was not their cup of tea.

At the beginning of fourth grade, the parents of my friend Meg started to push back against the notion that we could talk to spirits through the Ouija board. When Meg asked me to bring it to her house so we could play, they sat next to us in the dining room and told us that ghosts were not real and that the Ouija board only worked because one of us was pushing the indicator.

I told them that it was real. They laughed, told me I was dumb for believing that, and, in the course of our conversation, called me a liar multiple times.

Finally, they challenged me: "If you really want to prove that ghosts are real, leave the Ouija board on the table in the front porch and go play. If it moves on its own, we'll believe you." Meg's parents placed the indicator on the word yes, and then we walked it to the porch and placed it on the table. Hurt by how many times they called me a liar, wanting to prove that ghosts were real, and scared that they would keep calling me a liar, I made the horrible decision to move the indicator to the letter M as we walked out the door. It was not my proudest moment, but at the time, I wasn't sure that one of the spirits would move it for me. William was the only one I trusted to move it, and I wasn't sure if he had followed me to Meg's house.

When we got back to the house, the indicator had been moved off othe M to the moon at the top. Meg's parents accused me of moving it. They treated me like a liar. I was heartbroken that they didn't believe me, but then again, I had lied initially by moving the indicator . . . even if it had moved again after we left. I left Meg's house feeling defeated and angry. I blamed myself for their disbelief and felt like I had made myself a liar in the process.

A few weeks later, Meg still had questions about the Ouija board. I confessed to her that I had moved the indicator to the letter M before we left the house but that I hadn't moved it to the moon. She believed me but was still questioning that there were really ghosts around us, so I assured her that I could prove it. She came over to my house and we bellied up to the kitchen table with the Ouija board. We had our red Kool-Aid in hand, complete with fancy straws to drink from. We asked William about ten thousand questions that afternoon.

"What's your name?" was always the first question. He would look at me and roll his eyes.

"Where do you live?"

"How old are you?"

He answered all of the questions, but after a while, Meg told me she still didn't believe he was real. After all, I could be pushing the indicator to spell out the words myself. I got a little defensive and blurted out, more boldly than before, "I can prove it!" Without hesitation, I asked William to show her that he was really there. We watched for any signs of movement around us, and I saw it was much harder for him to move physical objects than I had originally thought. But he didn't give up: he didn't want to let me down. As Meg said, "Nothing's happ—" William stepped up to the table, looked at me, and placed his hand on the straw in my glass.

"William, will you move the straw in my glass?" I asked, hoping that it was easier to move than the other objects in the room.

"I don't know if I can!" His voice wavered at the thought of failing at such a specific request, but after the bathroom incident, I knew he could do it. I smiled as it started to spin around, from anyone else's perspective, by itself. It wasn't just a quick flick of the straw either: he wanted to make sure Meg knew he was there, and he made two full circles around the inside of my glass with it. I beamed with pride. My buddy William did that for me! He squealed with joy, but I saw his exhaustion and my stomach turned. Then I looked at Meg.

Sheer terror flooded her face as she saw proof of what she believed was impossible. William's friend Jay stepped in to try to calm her, but it was obvious that she couldn't see him or hear him. She grabbed my arm so tightly that I could barely feel my fingers, and her nails jabbed my wrists like a torture device.

I realized that in my haste to prove my honesty, I had done a terrible disservice to William and to Meg. Without regard for the consequences, I'd brought her full-steam-ahead into my world: a world that she didn't understand and was scared to admit existed. A world that her parents flat-out told her was not real. A scary world that had become so ingrained into my own life that I had trained myself to forget that the emotion I felt was fear. Meg released my arm and left my house as fast as she could.

I called after her, "It's okay!" trying to muster up the calming voice that my parents used with me when I was scared. But there was no convincing her that it was okay—for her, it wasn't.

I was very conflicted after Meg fled my house. On one hand, she couldn't call me a liar (even if her parents still did). On the other hand, she didn't want to come to my house anymore because she was afraid of the ghosts. After that, we didn't speak as much. I think she was afraid of what would happen when I was around. Other kids in our class, even those who were my friends, started acting strangely toward me as well. I started to hear the words *weird* and *crazy* thrown around the classroom more often. Though they weren't directed at me, I was more aware of the terms.

Jay started to talk to me more after that. Like a parent would, he reassured me that everything would be okay, and I believed him. However, I stopped asking the spirits to do things to prove they were there. I didn't want anyone to be scared, and I didn't want to lose friends.

4

BASEMENTS

Nothing in life is to be feared; it is only to be understood. Now is the time to understand more, so that we may fear less.
—Marie Curie

I have been in a lot of basements in my thirty-six years on this earth. Many scared me enough to turn me into a full-fledged marathon runner in just under four seconds. There is just something about the cold, dank feel on my skin, the smell of something foul that has been rotting in the walls for years without being discovered, and the eerie noises in the pipes and ductwork. It can send shivers down my spine strong enough to cause an earthquake. I don't like it; never have, never will.

It started, in this lifetime anyway, with the house on Thomas Ave. My parents owned and rented out this house in St. Paul until I was around ten years old. It was built in 1898, and in the years we lived there the neighborhood was plagued by drugs, theft, and prostitution. (A great place for children: I have no idea why my parents moved.) As a kid, I was never scared of the area or the people in the area. I was too naïve to notice the creeps walking past me or the drug deals going on in plain sight. I did, however, notice every house that had a spirit looking out the window at me as we walked to the corner gas station for soda, and I definitely noticed the creepy feeling of the basement in our house. The space reeked of moist dirt, mildew, rotting wood, and d-CON mousetraps, not to mention another smell that we could never quite place. Jessi and I, at the wise ages of ten and twelve, decided it was dead bodies.

The basement door opened from the kitchen onto the steps. After the top step the stairs turned to the right, and a ledge holding the mousetraps, random tools, and work gloves ran along the wall even with the top of that step. The walls were made of concrete block and stone, but were more concrete patching than either. To the right of the bottom of the stairs, beneath a couple of bare light bulbs, a creepy half wall taunted you to look over it and see whose body was hidden back there. I wasn't tall enough to see over it and neither was Jessi, but we felt our assumption about dead bodies was not unwarranted. Behind it was the source of the mysterious odor.

I never wanted to be left alone in that basement. There were people down there. They talked to me. I tried to ignore them, and succeeded until the day I was left down there by myself to clean up after yet another tenant trashed the house. Cleaning was always a family project, and this time I drew the short straw and got the basement.

I was bent over, sweeping with a hand broom under the steps. My back was to the half wall, and I was nervous that someone would crawl over it. I listened to what I could only assume were mice scurrying behind it. When I heard footsteps, my heart began to pound. Someone was coming up behind me! When I swung around, I stood face-to-face with an extremely pale, very plain fortyish woman in a long, gray skirt and a white blouse. She had dark hair and blinked her deep brown eyes at me.

"Hello," she said in a fairly stern, hushed, librarian-like voice.

My eyes widened, and I dropped the broom and dustpan. A plume of dust filled the air and recoated the floor that I had just swept. I did an about-face and scrambled up the stairs as quickly as I could. My dad and my cousin were in the kitchen, and the back door of the house was wide open. I considered running out of the house but then stopped at the top of the stairs, looking at my dad.

Earlier in the day I had been trying to get out of working in the basement, so my dad was already irritated with me. It showed on his face and in his voice when he asked, "What are you doin'?" His tone said that he was not in the mood to deal with my panic about the woman in the basement. I scurried back down the stairs without a word. I was on high alert the rest of the day, but the woman never returned.

Looking back, I am afraid that I hurt her feelings. It's too bad I didn't know then what I know now. Our "conversation" might have been very different. I could have learned about the history of the house, who lived there, and what that awful smell was. I hope it wasn't her.

I had no reason to fear many of the spirits that I saw as a child, but I had no frame of reference and no one to walk me through Psychic Medium 101. I walked around with a constant underlying sense of terror for reasons I didn't understand. I now know that the fear, more often than not, wasn't warranted. Most of the spirits that I see on a regular basis are just people who want to be heard. They have a message for their loved ones or are confused and need someone to guide them to the light. But I was alone and scared, though I tried to hide it, and I still didn't know why.

5

WHY IS MY GRANDPA IN YOUR BATHTUB?

In a dark time, the eye begins to see.
—Cavett Robert

When my friends came to my house, I would tell them stories about the energies in the basement: the people that I saw and the "itchy gods" in my dad's workshop.

Our basement wasn't completely finished. It had one bedroom, a dimly lit bathroom, a laundry room, a storage area, and my dad's workshop. The workshop filled about a third of the space with tools, workbenches, old locking cabinets, scrap wood, lots of sawdust, an eight-track player, and most notably, a creepy metal statue.

The statue was a six-inch dog created from miniature wrought-iron tools. It lived on a shelf between the Steppenwolf eight-track tape and the old coffee containers filled with screws. Of all the things in my life that freaked me out, this statue should not have made my list, but it did.

Even so, I begged my parents to let me move into the basement bedroom. I wanted to prove to myself and everyone else that I was a big kid. Unstoppable. Invincible. Unafraid. With a bit of coaxing, my parents let me take over the third of the basement on the other side of the stairwell from my dad's workshop. It had no door or carpet.

Evenings became even more eventful, but now I was acting out my fabricated sense of fearlessness. The statue sat on its shelf on the opposite side of the room, taunting me. I could feel the energy from the statue—or, at least, I thought it was from the statue. New figures appeared in my room at night and stood over my bed, silent and lurking. I would lie in bed, skin crawling and itching as if a military formation of ants were marching up and down my body. The dark figures didn't bother me as much as the itching did; I scratched every last centimeter of my body raw. I decided to name them the itchy gods.

I found importance in having a story to go along with the itchy gods. I didn't understand them, and it made me uncomfortable. I felt I needed something to tell my friends, and creepy, dark, and lurking figures didn't qualify as a good enough story in my mind. In order to liven up the tale a bit, I told my friends that the statue was the symbol of the itchy gods. If they started to itch at night and gave in to scratch, the itchy gods would steal their souls. (To my knowledge, all my childhood friends still have their souls, and I am pretty sure I kept mine, regardless of my continual scratching.)

After a year of the itchy gods invading my space, I stopped talking about them and started ignoring them as they lurked around my room at night. They disappeared not long after that. I now know that they gave up on delivering their messages through me and moved on to someone who could help them. For the most part, I forgot about them until a friend came over and checked to make sure the dog statue hadn't moved. My friends probably haven't forgiven me for the stories I told. I will admit now, though I wouldn't then, that I was a brat when it came to this story.

Basements and bathrooms seemed to be busy places for me as a child. Put them together, and I would avoid them like I avoid giant wolf spiders in the woods. The bathroom by my basement bedroom was unfinished. The walls were framed out but had no sheetrock. The toilet was a 1970s harvest gold color, and the bathtub stood on end, waiting to be installed. It was a source of fear for both me and my friend Sarah.

Sarah and I met in first grade and became best friends almost immediately. We had sleepovers (even on school nights), walked to A&W to get root beer floats, climbed over parked trains together, created our own languages, squealed about the boys that we were going to marry, and designed the elaborate home we were going to live in when we got old together. It had a library on one end for her, an art studio on the other for me, and a teleportation device in the middle so that we didn't have to walk far to see each other in our ten-thousand-square-foot mansion. Along with the fun times, we also had our share of childhood spats that usually ended after a day or two of not talking.

We still know each other better than most people, but until I was older, I didn't know how scared she was when I told her what was in my basement bathroom. By this time, I was so numb to the fact that others didn't see dead people that I thought I was helping when I told her. She was sleeping over at my house as she often did. Her grandfather had passed away a month before; I hadn't yet lost anyone in my family, so I didn't really understand the human grief process. To me, dying meant you could walk through walls, see whomever you wanted, and scare people on occasion. It wasn't necessarily a bad thing. I hadn't experienced loss the way Sarah had.

I had never met Sarah's grandfather, but I knew what he looked like from the pictures in her house. Naturally, when I saw him standing in the tub in our basement bathroom, I was excited to meet him! I was even more excited to tell her that he was still around. I ran up the stairs, through the kitchen, and down the hall to where Sarah was. I blurted, "Your grandpa is in the bathtub in the basement! He says hi!"

Her eyes grew wide, and she walked out of the room and down the hall with me in tow. I stopped in the kitchen as she continued down the basement stairs to go look in the bathroom.

Her head was filled with nightmarish images of her grandfather's decomposing corpse, flesh falling off the bones as he waited for her in the basement bathroom. She took the first few stairs down and stopped. Fear filled her body. After a few minutes, she stormed back up the stairs.

I was excited to ask her about her talk with her grandpa. What I got was completely unexpected.

"Why did you say that?" she demanded angrily.

I replied, "Because your grandpa said to tell you hi." I was confused about her question and her anger.

She repeated, "Why did you say that?" Her voice was bigger than before, more harsh and accusing.

My confusion grew. I thought, *Why is she yelling at me? Isn't she happy to see him?* She turned and stomped off. She collected her stuff and walked out the door. Her house was a mile and a half away. Distressed, I sat on our front step, crying, William on one side of me and Jay on the other.

Shortly after she left, she came back and asked my parents to drive her home. We didn't talk about it then, but a few days later, things were back to normal in our friendship. We had both swept it under the rug.

In our late teens, we briefly talked about how scared she was by that moment. I started to reflect on the impact of my experiences on the children around me. How many of the children in my class were traumatized by my "stories" growing up? Also, what in the world did the adults in my life think, and why didn't anyone tell me to stop talking about these things? I often wonder what I would have done had I known at the time that she'd had nightmares with horrible images of her grandfather since his death. Those images came crashing in when I said that he was in my basement. Could I have convinced her that he looked healthy and happy? Would it have helped her nightmares? Did her grandfather show up that day to help her understand or to help me understand?

Before that realization, I had pushed aside the inklings that others didn't see what I saw; I didn't fully believe that they couldn't see. I had no idea the effect that sharing my life would have on other people. When I found out that my experience was scary for Sarah, I began to understand that other people didn't see or hear dead people in the way that I did. I was also old enough to start to understand more of the complex emotions the spirits showed and some of the stories they wanted to share. However, I still wasn't convinced that I was the only one, and I wished that I knew someone else who could see and hear what I did.

Up until this point, I was fairly oblivious to other people's thoughts specifically about me. But that word, that horrible c-word, *crazy*, was now being thrown around the playground more often. The word sent shockwaves through my body. I started to feel fear again. I pressed the internal mute button over and over again in hopes that I could hide my fear of being labeled crazy. Kids would twirl a hand around their ears when I passed by, as if scrambling their brains with an imaginary eggbeater. And I started to see that gesture and that word used to describe me.

MESSAGES OF CLARITY

Sometimes, especially as children, we do not realize that our reality is not that of everyone around us. At times our intuitive gifts and psychic abilities allow us to feel emotions and know things that others don't understand or know how to express yet. This is called psychic empathy.

This ability can create sticky situations and misunderstandings if we don't know how to interpret what we are receiving. Have you ever made an assumption about another person's reality based on a feeling that you had? For example, have you assumed that someone is having a bad day because he or she "just doesn't feel right" to you? Have you had a feeling that something is wrong and called a friend to check in on them? Both situations are examples of intuition or psychic gifts being utilized to give us clarity on a situation.

When we aren't fully aware of or don't fully trust our gifts, we often allow our own human ego (thought, emotions, and experiences) to get in the way and cause miscommunication. When you have a feeling or receive an image, ask the following questions to gain clarity on whether the information coming through is from your ego or from your psychic senses or empathy gifts. If the answer to any of these questions is yes, you may be dealing with ego rather than your intuition.

1. Does this situation remind me of other situations I have experienced? If so, am I assuming the outcome of this situation will be the same?

2. Has the person, place, or thing I am sensing information about given me reason in the past or present to think this outcome would be likely?

3. Do I have a stake in the outcome of this situation?

4. Do I have a learned belief system around this situation? (This often occurs with topics that are controversial or stem from religious belief.)

5. If you have ruled out ego, can you make certain whose emotions you are feeling?

6. Is the emotion you are feeling yours?

7. Do you have a reason to feel this emotion? If you do not have cause to feel an emotion, it may not be yours.

8. Is there someone around you who is experiencing outward signs of this emotion or going through a life event that would cause this emotion?

If you determine that the emotion belongs to someone else, take a few moments to relax and ask your guides for assistance in removing the energies that do not belong to you. You can also use this information to offer support to the person to whom the emotions belong.

6

KITCHEN CLATTER

To effectively communicate, we must realize that we are all different in the way we perceive the world and use this understanding as a guide to our communication with others.
—Tony Robbins

I spent a lot of time at my grandparents' house as a kid. Whenever my parents went out of town for the weekend or needed a break from their wonderful daughters, I would visit my grandparents' house and Jessi would go to my aunt and uncle's house. (We must have been too much to handle together.) On weekends, my grandparents would take me to the St. Paul Farmers' Market and let me choose one thing I wanted. I had a flair for choosing the oddest thing I could find.

My first choice was a hand-carved bird a little bigger than a golf ball. It was attached to small, round slices of tree branch and smelled of the pine it was made from. Scales from pinecones made up its feathers, and the rest of the details were rendered in minimal detail. It felt earthy, and I connected with it immediately even thought I thought it was a bit ugly.

The next market trip took place the day before I left for Girl Scout camp. My grandma told me to pick out something to bring for a snack, and I chose, of all things, kohlrabi and jicama. I never had either before that day. I just liked the names; they sounded like fun. We went back to the house, cut it all up, and put it in little zippy bags. For the first few days, I was excited to enjoy something new and share something different with my friends. But I grew tired of my eccentric choices. The other kids were puzzled by my choice of snacks. They started to call me, and my snacks, weird.

Their taunting was exacerbated when I was asked to be in a group of four to pick the prayer for lunch. My camp counselor told me that I had to say the prayer. I felt like an outsider when I told the group I hadn't ever said grace before. "You've never said grace? What is wrong with you?" one of the other girls said. I shrugged. "Don't you go to church?" she continued.

A lengthy conversation about God and evolution ensued between fourth graders. The conversation ended with me sitting on a tree stump, surrounded by the other girls. One girl shouted, "My mom says that people who don't go to church are going to hell." Another chimed in with, "You are going to hell!" I had already heard this out of the mouths of aunts, uncles, and cousins for years.

Jay stepped in. With his hand on my shoulder he whispered adamantly in my ear, "That is not true."

I grew up hearing that I was going to hell because I listened to heavy metal music, because my family didn't go to church, because I thought that evolution sounded feasible, because, because, because. The words from these fourth graders' mouths didn't surprise me. It was what I expected when I was told I had to say grace. Somehow I was prepared for that moment, and Jay's words gave me the confidence to stay strong in my beliefs. I had faith that God was with me even if I didn't go to church or fully understand religion and even if I thought evolution could be true. My faith had nothing to do with church and everything to do with the spirits who supported me every day.

I left camp with a stronger sense that I didn't quite fit in. Somewhere deep down, I knew that everything I could see was preparing me for something bigger. I was being readied for something that was mine and that no one else could take from me. I wasn't okay with the judgment or the loneliness I felt, but somehow, I knew that Jay was going to help me through it.

The "something bigger" kept growing. I wasn't just seeing ghosts in my house or my friends' houses anymore. They were everywhere, including my grandparents' house.

When I stayed at their house, I slept on the couch in the living room. In the middle of the night I would wake up to see and hear someone walking around in the kitchen. At first I thought my grandparents were really thirsty people who got up about ten times a night, but then I realized that those people weren't my grandparents. A familiar sensation grew in the pit of my stomach: it was the same sensation that I felt at home. That was when I knew the ghosts were at their house, too.

"Can we keep the light on in the kitchen?" I asked my grandpa as I prepared for bed. He grumbled a bit of a yes but then turned it off when he went to bed, after I was asleep. I woke up that night, of course, and squinted at the dark shapes, narrowing my vision in hopes that they were shadows from a standing fan or a chair. But standing fans and chairs can't walk, and I had to admit to myself that there were ghosts in the kitchen. I closed my eyes as tight as I could, pulled the blankets over my head, and wished that I wouldn't feel their presence anymore. Each time I visited, I hoped that they wouldn't stand over my makeshift bed or pull on the covers like William did at home. Mostly, I hoped they would ignore me and continue with their normal routine. They didn't know that I could see them, and they ignored me until the night I decided it was rude to continue ignoring them.

That particular night, I was extremely sensitive to the spirit activity in the house and became more and more anxious lying on the couch. My eyes burned as I tried to force them closed. I was beyond tired, but every part of my body was on high alert. I heard the dainty footsteps of a woman walking across the kitchen floor and then the loud, masculine footsteps that could only be from heavy work boots on the hardwood floor. I looked up toward the kitchen and saw two shadows. I lay awake for hours, trying to ignore them, but I could still hear them even when I did get my eyes to close. I wanted to go to sleep, but now everything in me wanted to see who those people were.

I got up to turn on the light in the kitchen, hoping to alleviate my fear. Light usually helped me to see the whole person, the whole spirit. With the lights off, it felt sinister. The figures would morph and change like the last snowman of winter on a warm day. In the dark, even the most beautiful spirit on Earth was a shadow that moved like the wind and changed shape depending on the reflection of the small amount of light from the moon through the window.

I walked into the kitchen. The two figures stopped and looked at me. I had startled them. "Who are you?" the woman quietly asked. I didn't want to talk; I just wanted the light on so I could get to sleep. I ignored them, flipped the light switch on, and got a good look at them in the light.

She looked like a homemaker, and it was obvious that they didn't have means. She wore a faded pink pastel dress that was worn at the seams and slightly frayed along the bottom. Her hair was perfect if you looked from the front, but the back of her head was slightly matted, like she couldn't reach to finish curling it. Her makeup had worn off during the day, which gave her a more natural look and revealed light wrinkles. Her features were worn like her dress and more asymmetrical than most people's. Yet, something about the way that she carried herself was uniquely beautiful and caught my attention.

He looked as if he had just returned from a shift at the factory. His clothing was dirty and stained, but not from lack of care. His fingernails were decorated with speckles of grease and his hands saturated in it. His hair was the color of coal, but I was unsure if it was from the grease that coated him or if it was his natural hair color. *Rough* barely described his look. The more that I watched him, the more I realized his roughness was more about survival than his attitude toward life. It was obvious he was a provider for his family. He had a strong sense of responsibility, and he carried himself in a way that made that apparent, even to me as a kid. His roughness faded when he interacted with his wife. An incredibly kind and caring softness came over his face then, completely dissolving the roughness of his appearance.

When I saw them in the light, I felt obliged to be more cordial, even though I was exhausted. I nodded to them and quietly said, "Good night." Their eyes grew wide and their mouths dropped open. I am not sure if it was shock that there was a child in their house or shock that I could see them. Obviously, this was a first for them. However, it was just the beginning of our late-night talks and the other chatter at my grandparents' house.

As I think about it, the spirits didn't belong to the house. The house wouldn't have been there when they were alive. They were just there. Maybe they were sent by spirit or God to teach me something about my gifts, or maybe they just felt at home there. Of all the spirits I saw as a child, these two held a key that opened a door to gifts that I had not yet touched. They did not instill fear in me like the others did, and it felt as if their love for each other reached further than the ends of time. I couldn't help but feel the love that they shared for each other and, in time, for me. They accepted me for who I was, the weird little girl who could see them. I loved to watch them interact with each other, although I think they were slightly embarrassed when they first realized that I could see them.

These gentle souls surrounded me with love for years. Each time I walked in the door at my grandparents' place, they smiled and nodded to acknowledge I was there. Their presence gave me reason to believe I didn't always have to be afraid of the spirits around me. "How was your day?" they would ask when I sat down. They once shared, "We never had children. It is nice to have you here." I didn't understand why they wouldn't have had kids of their own, but I was more than willing to be a stand-in.

The more time that I spent with this couple, and with Jay and William, the more comfortable I was hearing messages from the other spirits that popped in and out of my life. I still felt fear, but I was getting better at pushing the mute button.

MESSAGES OF CLARITY

As I looked back on my snack choices of kohlrabi and jicama for camp, I recognized that they illustrate portions my life as a medium. My choices sounded perfect in the beginning, but as other people's views seeped in, my perception changed and I tired of my own choices as well as the judgment of others around me. As a medium, the judgment of others kept me in a state of fear. Recognition of my own fear and the realization that it was tiresome and limiting freed me to develop and use my gifts.

1. Where, in your life, have you noticed your choices changing as you start to learn more about yourself and grow?

2. Where have you noticed that you felt pushed to make changes based on what other people were telling you? How do those changes make you feel?

Have you given yourself space to explore your options and reflect on your choices? What did you learn from your reflections?

7

AFTER-SCHOOL PROGRAMMING

> *Walking with a friend in the dark is better than walking alone in the light.*
> —Helen Keller

I had a lot of friends in school, but I always felt alone with them. Many didn't understand me, and I was becoming more and more aware that I couldn't share all my experiences with them. Some days, I just wanted to go home. In elementary school I often faked feeling sick so I could go home and play with my cats. I could tell them anything. My parents both worked: my mom before and after school, and my dad all day long. Normally, Jessi and I were home alone for three hours after school.

On the days that I went home sick, I usually had about an hour between when my mom left for work and when Jessi got home. The older neighbor in the house behind us would check in on me then, or I would go to her house. She was legally blind but still had enough eyesight to play cards with me. She fed me cinnamon sugar sandwiches with sugar chunks the size of horse pills and an unlimited supply of Fudgesicles. If I wasn't sick before going over there, I probably should have been after all that sugar!

On the days she didn't check in on me, I was alone. Most children I knew would have watched TV during this time. Not me.

The house was extremely active with spirits at that time of the day. The La-Z-Boy chair rocked by itself, I heard footsteps down the hallway, people talked in the basement, and William chattered at me incessantly. When I ignored him he would get so upset with me that his eyes would squint and darken and his face would turn red. Then he'd throw a full-on, little-kid-in-the-toy-store temper tantrum, screaming, "Why don't you want to see me anymore? When do I get to come see you again for real?" It wasn't often that he yelled, but it got under my skin and made me cautious about what I said to him. I had no idea who he was, why he was always with me, or what he meant by "for real." But, annoying as he could be, he was my stability. He was my reset button. He was one of the only spirits that I felt I really knew, and if he was there, I felt safer than if he were not.

One day when I was home sick, the La-Z-Boy recliner in the living room jolted to life and started rocking on its own while I was sitting in it. My heart beat like the hooves of a racehorse vying for first place in the Triple Crown. I let out the tiniest of screams and tried to rationalize it.

Option one: One of the cats had jumped onto the back of the chair and jumped off again, springing the rocker to life. I scanned the room for my cats. Both were fast asleep on the other side of the room, peaceful and completely clueless about what had just happened.

Option two: A ghost shook the chair to scare me. I had no way to rule this option out. I looked around the room and saw nothing, but I could feel that they were present. One by one they showed themselves to me: faces that I didn't know, strange new spirits who were just swinging on through to say hello. I was surrounded, but none of them admitted to rocking the chair.

Last but not least, option three: THERE WAS NO OPTION THREE!

Overwhelmed and confused why no one was fessing up, I booked it to the nearest flat surface I could find: the kitchen floor. I sat with my back against the cabinets, crying. The cabinets were hard and cold, but they felt safe for the moment. Images from the book *Scary Stories to Tell in the Dark* flashed in my head. I thought, *Ghosts can walk through walls. . . . if they can walk through walls, then they can certainly sneak up behind me through the cabinets, even if my back is against them.*

I worried that a ghost was going to pop out of the cabinet and grab me. I shuffled my body back and forth to look over each shoulder. *Oh good, nothing there. WAIT, what was that noise?* I turned around to look over the opposite shoulder, relaxed, and then freaked myself out again. The cabinet door opened slightly every time I turned and slammed as I shifted again. Naturally, I thought it was a ghost.

I cried even harder. Questions filled my head: *What do I do if a ghost grabs me? Why won't they tell me who pushed the chair?*

William crouched on the floor next to me, asking, "Why are you scared? What's wrong?"

I shrugged my shoulders and sobbed, "I don't know." I cried until my sister came home.

When I failed to be fearless, I found only two ways to cope with this fear: hold on to my cats for dear life because I knew that somehow they would protect me, or avoid being alone at home. Most of the time, I chose the latter.

I had several friends who lived within blocks of our house. I started going to their houses after school. Most of their parents weren't home either, so it gave my friends a reprieve from their empty houses as well. We ordered Bigfoot pizzas from Pizza Hut with money we found in our couch cushions and made prank phone calls; the best part was that I didn't have to worry about the ghosts in my cabinets!

After a while I started pushing my mute button more frequently. I elaborated on the fearless narrative I had been writing in my head. It stifled my fear more and more with each passing year and each new spirit encounter. I wanted to be fearless. I wanted to be "normal." But I wasn't. I still turned on every light as I walked through the house, and most of the time, I ran through rooms like someone was chasing me with a giant knife, especially if I was coming up from our basement.

8

WHEN SOMETHING DOESN'T SEEM RIGHT, IT PROBABLY ISN'T

> *Hope is not a form of guarantee; it's a form of energy,*
> *and very frequently that energy is strongest*
> *in circumstances that are very dark.*
> —John Berger

Every year on my birthday, we had a birthday party at my house, and afterward I spent the night (sometimes the weekend) at the home of my mom's friend, Denise. It was a tradition. We celebrated with a gourmet dinner of macaroni and cheese from the box, loaded with sliced hotdogs or tuna from the can. The smell of powdered cheese and tuna still brings me back to those moments. It was one of my favorite meals. Well, anything with hotdogs or macaroni and cheese was my favorite meal.

Denise lived in a few different places when I was growing up, but the most memorable was an old house in St.Paul. I was in sixth grade at the time and remember telling stories of this house while I watched the other kids play spin the bottle in our classroom. The girls squawked and screamed as I told the stories. I was never sure if they were scared or just upset about who they had to kiss.

As we drove up to Denise's house for our first tour after she moved in, I looked out the back window and saw her neighbor creeping down his driveway in a manner that was gracefully disjointed. His feet shuffled across the pebbled ground like he was a child kicking rocks down the road on his way to school.

His hunched body swayed slightly from side to side with each step, like a lookout tower swaying in a strong wind. His chin was tucked down to his chest, but his eyes focused ahead. He looked up at us with a hollow expression as we passed. I felt like I was looking at a character from the movie *The 'Burbs* and played out scenarios in my head of what he did at night in his house. All of them involved murder and burying bodies. He gave me the chills. As I looked closer, the fragility of his gaunt body made me doubt that murder and burials were a possibility. His ashen skin suggested that he rarely came out in the light of day, and it was so thin that I would later tell people that he was see-through. I thought, *If I touch him, his skin might fall off*. His presence was just the first of many bone-chilling moments to come. In fact, he was far less scary than the man in Denise's house.

Walking into the house that first time, my skin crawled. Something didn't feel right. I wished that William were there to help me figure out what it was.

It wasn't until Denise brought us to the basement that I knew why I felt so weird about the house. We walked down the steps into another world, one I wanted nothing to do with. I started getting short, cryptic flashes of images that no kid should ever see. Every bit of me knew what I was seeing was real. With each step down, the fear grew stronger and the images more intense. I saw torture and rituals that I didn't understand. I heard voices that didn't sound human and screams so vividly human that I wanted to plug my ears and scream to drown them out.

I was getting used to random visions then, but this was different. My stomach churned, my eyes burned at the gruesome sights, and my ears felt as if they were going to start bleeding from the sounds. This series of images felt truly evil. As we looked around the basement, I started to drown the images out with a slew of internal questions.

We approached the bottom of the stairs and turned to face a wall that was bizarrely decorated with toilet seats. I felt drawn to them, like I was being beckoned to open them. As much as I didn't want to, I stretched out my arm and lifted one of them. I was inundated with visions. I heard those voices again and saw what I can only describe as a portal, a swirling mass of darkness and light all mixed together, screaming in my face while at the same time surrounding me. It was like a combination of the background in the paintings *Starry Night* and *The Scream*, but with a splash of Satan and a hint of hell for added effect.

As a kid, I had no way of knowing about other dimensions or any of the things that I saw there. I later described it to the children in my class as "a portal to another place . . . a very bad place." I opened the next lid, hoping for a scene to erase the one before. It only got darker and more encompassing. I slammed it shut and tried the next, and then the next, losing more of my childhood with each one. The visions took my breath away. In one I could see the souls of hundreds of human beings engulfed in flames, screaming as they were tortured by creatures that I didn't recognize and didn't *want* to recognize. I felt paralyzed, like I couldn't look away. I wanted to close my eyes. The face of a large, horned, gargoyle-like creature started to move toward me, but I felt Jay come up behind me. The creature recoiled, and I felt its anger toward him. Jay took my hand and helped me close the lid. His eyes focused on mine, and I heard the usual gentleness in his voice as he said, "I think you have seen enough." I wanted to run screaming up the stairs, but how do you tell your family that there is evil in the house? Jay seemed saddened by what I had seen, but he smiled at me anyway, laid his hand on my back, and guided me to the left, in the direction of my parents.

Jay was different from the other spirits. I felt nothing but love from him, and he always showed up when I needed comfort and protection. I wondered who he actually was.

The toilet seats from hell had pulled me away for only a few minutes, though it felt far longer, and I came back to hear Denise say in her best Minnesotan accent, "I know, isn't it crazy?" I looked up, still in shock, and saw everyone staring at a giant table next to the wall. My body was trembling, and I was trying to get my head back to what I was hoping would be a much more normal reality.

"Maybe they used it to hang their laundry," I heard someone say. This table was enormous. The legs were at least six feet tall. I started to feel woozy as I looked at it; my skin crawled again, and I started to itch. The itching made me feel safe and comfortable for a brief moment. I started to think about the itchy gods, and then I realized my parents were standing under that table. I wanted to yell, "DON'T STAND UNDER THERE!" but no words would come out of my mouth. I stared at it, then at the toilet seats, and then back to the table.

"I think we are just going to cut off the legs and use it to fold laundry," Denise said matter-of-factly. My brain was spinning. I kept repeating in my head, "But they used it for bad things! You can't!"

We continued our basement tour and I tried to shut out the noises, the vision, and the whirling, nauseous thoughts. The last room I remember was the most awful place I have ever been. It was damp and so dark that I'm not sure if it had any lights at all. It had typical cinder-block walls and a floor so cold that I am certain water would freeze on it. The detail I remember most was the chains and ankle cuffs attached to the wall. I don't know if they were physically there or if the images were just imprinted in the energy of the room. The thick chains elicited images of people tethered to the wall, screaming and fighting to break free. Again, images that no kid should have in their mind.

I hated that basement, and in that moment, I didn't like the way that my brain worked either. These images made me feel crazy, twisted, and sick. I started to fear that I was a bad person on the inside. I remember telling people about the toilet seats on the wall and the swirling energy in them, the howls that I heard, the chains, and the giant table. No one questioned it; no one told me that I had an overactive imagination, and now that I think about it, there is no way that anyone was truly listening to the words coming out of my mouth.

At the time, I was convinced no one would believe me if I talked about the worst of the images I saw, so I stuffed the terrifying details in a box way in the back of my brain. Only the sound of the howls and screams remained etched in my conscious mind. They have been forever present. I described the howls to kids at school when we were telling spooky stories. That was as far as I went. I knew that the awful c-word might come out of someone's mouth if I went any further. However, this terrifying experience was also one of the first to help prepare me for the healing work I do now. Once you have seen the evil that resides in the world, you can recognize it in all forms and help people heal from it.

The first night I spent at that house, Denise, her husband, and I watched a movie in the living room. I was creating my own lightning storm with a plasma ball toy. I watched each lightning bolt connect with my fingertips as I lightly stroked the top of the orb. Then, out of the corner of my eye, I saw someone walk past me. I looked up and saw an old man in a black suit walk through the living room. Glancing over at me, he gave me a creepy smile and walked down the hall with an antique skeleton key on display in his hand. I looked around the room to see if anyone else was looking at him. No one so much as glanced in his direction. I was on my own, again, seeing people that weren't there. I hoped that I wasn't crazy.

Later that night I was told that my room was up in the attic. I was relieved that it wasn't in the basement, but the attic wasn't a lot better. The problem was twofold. First, my bed was surrounded by little cupboards, and after years of dealing with cupboards at home, I didn't want to subject myself to one night of them. Second, the light switch was at the bottom of the stairs on the opposite side of the attic from my bed. There was only one way to get through this. I stood at the bottom of the stairs with the door closed tightly behind me and counted the number of stairs going up to the attic: one, two, three, four . . . sixteen steps. I placed my hand on the light switch, closed my eyes, flipped the switch off, and ran like a mouse fleeing from a cat up the stairs and across the attic. The bed slid a few inches across the floor as I dove in and, as quickly as I could, yanked the sheets over my head and cupped my hands over my ears to drown out the chatter that I knew was about to begin. There was no light to soften the fear of what was in the dark, and there were no parents to come to my room if I cried. I laid there for hours trying to sleep, trying not to listen to the noises of the house, not to remember how many cupboards surrounded my bed or think about what might come out of each of those cupboards if I closed my eyes. I could hear the footsteps of people walking around the bed but saw nothing. I was completely blinded by the darkness, and my mute button was broken. Eventually, exhaustion took hold and I fell asleep. I woke up only to dread doing it all over again the next night.

My dread scattered itself throughout my day but remained intact. Playing in the yard, Denise and I found an old skeleton key. As we picked it up, clumps of dirt and rust fell from the edges and I saw that it was the skeleton key that the man in the black suit had been carrying the day before. I asked what it was for, hoping there was an answer to explain where it came from. Playtime turned into a hunt for the door that this key unlocked. After checking every lock in the house, the shed, and the garage, we couldn't figure out what it unlocked. I flashed back to our first visit to the house. I remembered the shackles on the wall in the basement, and for a split second I wanted to tell Denise. I wanted to tell her about what I saw in the toilet seats, the images that were revealed as I looked at the table, and the man in the house, but by this point, I hesitated to tell adults about the things that I saw and heard. I was afraid that I was losing my mind. What would happen to me if I shared all the details?

Before I went upstairs that night, I got myself a glass of milk. I was stalling. I walked back toward the attic door, but before sprinting upstairs I looked out the window at the neighbor's house. The basement windows were glowing red. The light flashed on and off, and each time it did, I got a little more worried that the neighbor was killing people in the basement. However, I convinced myself it was a television and didn't dwell on that too long. I had much more concerning things to deal with: What was going to attack me from the cupboards by my bed? How could I shut off the light without having to run up the stairs like a wild cheetah? What could I use for a night-light? You know, the questions most kids ask before they go to bed.

I was standing there, preparing for the run up the steps, when I heard Denise ask, "Do you want me to shut the light off for you?"

I wanted to shout, "OH MY GOSH, YES!!! THANK YOU!" But instead I let out a meek, "Yes, please!" and grinned. A huge sigh of relief and momentary calm flooded over me. Denise walked with me up the steps.

She rambled on as I got settled in bed: "In the morning when you get up you can have cereal for breakfast. I put the cereal on the counter, and you know where the milk is." I felt relaxed and calm as she walked down the steps to shut off the light. The calm quickly faded as the room went dark. *Hello, darkness. We meet again.*

I knew I had a force larger than myself protecting me. I remembered Jay's promise at Girl Scout camp that I was not going to hell. The way the creature behind the toilet-seat portal had recoiled when it saw Jay walk up behind me was etched in my mind, creating an abundance of questions. I buried the images in a compartment in my brain but have never forgotten. The safety I felt when Jay was with me never faded either. I started to question who he was, and I finally decided to ask.

I questioned William, "How do you know him?"

He shrugged his narrow shoulders, "When it is scary, he helps."

I continued, "When did you meet him?"

"He held my hand when it got bright."

Not understanding, I repeated, "When?"

William's face lit up at the memory. "Jay is fun. He wants to be our friend. He wants us to be happy . . . not scared anymore. When it got bright he said his name is Jesus but . . . " He paused. "He said I can call him J."

I just sat there, staring at my companion. "J, not Jay. Jesus, not Jay."

My family didn't go to church, but other people had used Jesus against me. I was well aware of who the Jesus they talked about was, and he certainly didn't like me. He was not fun. He did not want me to be happy. He scared me. He was an angry and judgmental man. Jay could not be Jesus.

The taunting from camp rang out in my head: "You are going to hell!" followed by Jay's words, "That is not true." I thought about the way he'd tried to console my friend when she was scared about the Ouija board, the way he talked to William, and how the creature reacted in the basement. A plethora of conversations we'd had played through my head like a movie.

"This is not the same person," I said, thinking aloud. "This can't be the same person."

William's big eyes looked at me as I sat there, silent. He was confused about my sadness and my anger. I was confused about Jesus.

I was angry at myself for showing a moment of hope that Jesus, *the* Jesus, loved me, was there to protect me, and had actually told me that I wasn't going to hell. My hope turned to great anger as I decided Jay was lying. I was angry that he would lie to William by saying he was someone that he wasn't. That anger brought up resentment and also anger at certain members of my family for their continual judgment. I was angry at them for creating a sense of sin within me—one more thing to fear—and the illusion that I was an outcast for my beliefs. I judged them for judging me, which made me even angrier. In this moment, I was filled with hatred and confusion. *Who is Jesus?* I wondered. Was he the man of judgment and shame that I believed him to be, or was he the man of compassion and peace that William believed in?

Jay stood in the back of my room intently watching as William and I sat on the edge of my bed, talking. I didn't realize he was there at first, but when I finally looked up and saw him, my brow furrowed and the anger seeped from my eyes. He said nothing. He just looked at me calmly, with love. I felt better knowing he was there, but I wanted to hate him in that moment. I honestly believed that he had lied to William about who he was.

He walked toward us and sat down between William and me. William was elated to see him and gave him a giant hug. Jay smiled a heart-melting smile and put his hand on mine. It was warm and filled with compassion.

His tone was different than normal. The gentleness that he exuded was still present. However, his words were more earnest. They carried more weight than I had ever heard from him before.

"You know the truth. It has never changed."

I thought, *What the heck does that mean? Which truth? Are you the Jesus, or are you Jay?* My internal tone was harsh, rage-filled and sharp.

He heard the thought and smiled a half smile. He looked at me with a deeper gaze and repeated, "It has never changed."

I was afraid to believe what I felt was true. I blurted, "So, who are you?"

With that question, the Jay that I had come to know answered in a way that he knew I would understand. He used my words, "I am *the* Jesus." His smile widened, and I could see laughter in his eyes. I did know the truth. Nothing had changed. He had been walking with me and protecting me all these years.

My experiences in that house showed me a deeper level of my own faith and reminded me who was walking by my side. It helped me to see the faith that I must hold on to in order to use the gifts that have been given to me. That house was the catalyst that led me to ask more questions. Each day after that conversation, he spoke truth to me as only he could, with an amazing amount of compassion, grace, laughter, and complete honesty.

9

THE PITH AND THE PENDULUM

> *Change is the end result of all true learning.*
> —Leo Buscaglia

I wish I could say I approached everything after that moment with grace and compassion, but I didn't. There were times when I judged people so I didn't have to admit how strange I felt I was. I never wanted to accept that I was going to grow up to be "abnormal." In fact, the day I announced to my friends that I was going to school to be a massage therapist, they made me swear I would not be one of those weird, New Age massage therapists. Oops, guess I lied to them. None of those healing stones, crystals, pendulums, and scrying balls were real, right? They were, as far as I was concerned, hokey props for fake psychics and scam artists. If you are a real psychic, I thought, you "shouldn't" need those things.

In grade school, I didn't have anyone to talk to about my gifts or about the paranormal, so my beliefs were shaped by my own bizarre experiences, Hollywood portrayals, and cartoonish ideals on television. This created in me an impulse to judge others that now seems out of place and extremely hypocritical. As I have grown into my abilities, I see that judging others hindered my own growth, stifled my learning, and created doubt within myself.

The judging started when I was about twelve, the day my cousin Eileen and her neighbor, Sharla, introduced the pendulum to me. I remember my eye rolls and snide thoughts very well. We were all sitting on the floor in Sharla's bedroom. We weren't supposed to be in her house for some reason, so she had sneaked us in through the back door, and we kept one eye on the clock to make sure her dad wouldn't catch us. She had rock candy growing on the window ledge in between a few plants, books neatly stacked on bookshelves, and rocks tied to strings that she and Eileen were swinging around for, from what I could tell, no good reason.

With my eyebrows raised and a smirk in my heart, I wondered what they were doing and mentally checked out for a moment. As I looked around the room, the rock candy caught my attention. I remembered trips with my mom and Jessi to Candy Land in St. Paul. We would take the city bus, get off on the corner, and follow the brick pavers and benches to the store. We always begged my mom to buy us rock candy. As I sat on the floor, I couldn't help but think, *It grows in a jar on a stick?* I stared at it, enthralled, until Eileen talked to her rock.

This was my first exposure to pendulums, and for the entirety of the experience, I judged. They were fishing for answers to their problems. I judged them like people judged me and my Ouija board. But somewhere deep inside, I wanted to believe it was real.

Still, I asked, "How would a rock know the answer?" with a certain air of criticism in my voice.

Eileen and Sharla couldn't answer me with any sense of confidence. "It just does" they huffed back.

With the Ouija board, at least I knew the spirits were moving the indicator. I saw no spirits moving the pendulum. I thought it had to be fake and was quite clear about that to them.

They wanted to prove it to me, just as I had wanted to prove the Ouija board to Meg and her parents. Eileen started asking Sharla questions about herself that she wouldn't necessarily know how to answer unless divinely guided. They had to be yes-or-no questions, so I was unimpressed with her ability to guess the correct answers with 50/50 odds. I watched their hands to see if they were moving to force the rock in a specific direction. I analyzed their questions to see if they were making the questions easier to answer. Part of me hoped that they could prove it. The other part of me decided they were weirder than I was.

No proof that day changed my mind about that swinging rock. It wasn't until years later, when I was in massage school, that I finally saw the light. I was talking with my instructor about different types of massage and ways to listen to the body. He pulled out a dowsing-for-beginners book and handed it to me, saying, "It isn't for everyone, but I think you will find it interesting." When I got home, I flipped open the book. I was shocked to read about pendulums and the power of a lovely little rock on a string. Guilt took over my body as I thought about how I'd judged Eileen and Sharla seven years earlier. I repeated to myself, "I was wrong."

It turns out that science, historical knowledge, and metaphysical beliefs—none of which I would have understood when I was a kid—all explain the use of the pendulum. The book talked about the subconscious mind and nerve function, and how pendulums were used by doctors, scientists, and even the military to solve a multitude of different problems. They used pendulums to find infections and save lives, find buried bombs, and seek water for wells. Some people thought that angels controlled the pendulum's swing, while others thought that the vibration of the stone creates the movement. At that point, all I thought was, *You were so wrong!*

My experience with Eileen and Sharla was likely the pith of my learning. It was essential to the lesson "Judge not, lest ye be judged." After reading the book, I finally picked up my first pendulum. I received the same looks and the same judgment from some of my friends. They laughed until my swinging rock got the answers right. Luckily, I could also back them up with messages from my spirit friends.

MESSAGES OF CLARITY

There have been many moments in my own life when I looked back on a situation from a new point of view and saw the error in my previous thinking. Sometimes, I was not ready to admit the error of my thinking and remained stubborn in my view. Other times, I made the decision to accept my mistake and move forward with more knowledge.

As a kid I was curious about the pendulum; I wanted to believe but refused to allow myself to explore it, fearing that I would be wrong or labeled weird. My refusal to explore the possibility was a choice that I now feel stunted my spiritual growth. As I got older, I started to allow myself to try new things and admit my mistakes or whether something didn't work for me. This has helped me to find freedom in my decision making and allowed me to live free of judgment toward other people.

1. Where in your life have you denied yourself a new experience because of your own judgment of others or fear of judgment from others?

2. Which experiences can you try again?

3. Are you ready to let go of the old experience and try again?

4. List three things you will try again now that you have a different perspective.

10

MY LIFE SHOULD BE A SCARY MOVIE

You gain strength, courage, and confidence by every experience in which you really stop to look fear in the face. You are able to say to yourself, "I lived through this horror. I can take the next thing that comes along."
—Eleanor Roosevelt

As a kid, I hated taking showers. Far worse than anything hiding in the dark was what stood outside the curtain, waiting for me to close my eyes or turn my back. I had a fear of dying in the shower, and every time the light flickered or the curtain moved, I would whip open the shower curtain to make sure that no one was there.

I am not sure what I would have done if some strange being had actually appeared, but after years of preparing myself, I thought I would be ready to fight. I experienced this fear before going through the passing of a loved one or even witnessing a death on television, let alone a murder. There had to be an explanation for my feelings; fears like that don't usually appear out of nowhere.

At first, I would get in the shower, curl up in the corner, and just let the warm water run over me. I can't count how many times I had conversations with my parents about making sure I washed everything while I was in the shower. They had no idea how paralyzing my fear was. I don't think I ever talked about it.

Baths would have been a better option for me because I didn't get water in my eyes, which meant I didn't have to close them or turn my back to the shower curtain. I was under the impression that if something attacked me, it would be better if I could see it coming. (Now that I think about it, I'm not sure how that was better!) Even though I always had the option to take baths, I didn't want to admit my fear of taking showers. I was still trying to create the persona of fearless Jenni.

Eventually, I developed a shower ritual. I sat on the floor of the shower, as tight against the tub wall as I could, and washed everything, careful never to turn my back to the shower curtain. When I needed to wash my hair, I followed an invisible quadrant system on my head—left front, left back, right back, and right front—that ensured that the shower curtain was in full view for three-quarters of the task. The last quarter concluded with a mad rush to wash all the soap out of my hair without being murdered.

At the age of fourteen, I begged my parents to buy a removable shower head. I told them that it would make it easier to wash my hair. Really, it was so I never had to turn my back to the curtain. They obliged, and while my shower routine remained the same, I didn't have to rush through that last quadrant anymore. I thought this was how everyone lived. While I didn't like it, I thought this fear was normal until well into my teens.

As a teenager, I started to question why I was so scared but never came up with a concrete answer. For a while I thought maybe I could see the future and somehow knew I was going to die in the shower. This ramped up my fear and made me more diligent in my rituals. I played out potential scenarios in my head: What if someone came into the bathroom to kidnap me while I had my back turned? Which way would I turn? How would I grab their arm? Would I bite, scratch, claw, or punch my way out of their grip? I thought of every minute detail. I planned each time I stood in the shower, listening to the general noises of our bathroom; the floor creaking, the water moving through the pipes, and the vent fan blowing.

Then, one day, an unfamiliar noise broke my routine. I ripped the shower curtain open and caught a glimpse of a shadowy figure gliding through the door, out of the bathroom. I panicked. I scanned the room to make sure nothing else was in the bathroom with me. I was only halfway through my hair washing ritual, and soap was running down the right side of my face and into my eye. It burned, and I struggled to see through it. I couldn't stop my shower now, even if I was terrified. I reached for my towel, and what waited for me left me in a full-fledged, heart-beating-out-of-my-chest panic.

My towel, neatly folded on top of the closed toilet seat, was now decorated with a giant handprint. I tried to convince myself that it was mine, but as I laid my hand down on top of it, I saw it was twice the size. My stomach churned, my insides burned with fear, and my eyes started to well up. It was coming true; something was there to kill me. I knew it. My heart pounded so hard that I could not catch my breath. My throat started to close, and my hands shook like a Chihuahua on a cold day. Tears streamed down my face as I thought about my murderer, touching *my towel* in *my bathroom* as he plotted to kill me.

I ran my hand over the towel to erase the handprint in hopes that if I didn't see it anymore, I could believe that it wasn't ever there. I quickly closed the shower curtain, sat down in the corner, and washed the rest of my hair with my handheld sprayer. I prepared myself for the *fact* that someone or something was going to burst through the shower curtain. But they never came. The noises in the bathroom faded away, and eventually I caught my breath and stopped crying.

Later, I talked to William and learned that the shadow was just a spirit passing through. Nothing dark, no one who wanted to murder me, just a plain old spirit. Just another day in the shower. Questioning my own fears became more important to me that day. I didn't want to live in fear anymore. This also meant that my quest for answers became more important. One problem still remained: I didn't know anyone else like me. I had no one to go to with questions, and it would be many more years before I met a healer who would help me find my answers about my fear of showers.

MESSAGES OF CLARITY

1. What routines do you use to help calm your emotions or help you to feel safe in stressful situations?

2. What routines can you add in your life to assist you?

11

ANGEL FEATHERS AND FUNERALS

A feather is a sign from the angels. It is a response to a question, a thought or an emotion. It's their way of saying, "You are loved and are being guided through this by the angelic realm."
—Eileen Anglin

When I was in eighth grade my uncle was diagnosed with lung cancer. I don't remember our family talking much about it, but I do remember that even though he was going through chemo treatments and planning for the worst, he still did everything he could to help his friends and family.

I was oblivious to a lot that was going on around me at the time, stuck in my fourteen-year-old world of telephones, boys, and goofing off (when I wasn't worried about the ghosts). I talked on my corded hot pink, purple, and teal telephone for hours with my friends from school. We made up code names for the boys we talked about and euphemisms for semi-obscene topics that made us sound cool. We called boys from our class and hung up when they answered because we were too afraid to talk to them.

This time in my life was filled with friends who had been labeled in their own ways. Some were popular kids but didn't want to be; others grew up in the wrong part of town or were just too odd to be part of the cool crowd. Each of us had a story and a label. We overlooked the labels and stood by each other, and I found community despite the judgment.

Between phone calls I would hear my parents talking about my uncle.

He wasn't doing well. I could hear in my parents' voices that he was finishing up his time on this earth. When they went to the hospital, I stayed home and, in typical teenage fashion, called a friend as soon as they walked out the door. We didn't have call waiting on our phone at the time, so if someone was calling, I had no way of knowing.

An hour into my phone call, a white feather fell down from the ceiling and landed in the palm of my hand. It had never happened before, but I instinctively knew what it meant. Another person had been called home to be in the presence of the angels. My uncle had passed away.

I blurted to my friend, "A white feather just fell from the ceiling and into my hand . . . we don't have anything with feathers in our house."

"Oooooookaaayyyyy," she responded. "What does that m—"

The telephone operator interrupted her: "I am breaking into this telephone line because you have an important telephone call coming in." I didn't know they could do that! It had to be important.

Then I heard my cousin John's voice on the other end of the line. He said that he had been calling for a while and couldn't get through, so he called the operator. I let my friend go immediately, and John told me to have my parents call him as soon as they walked in the door. His tone confirmed what I already knew.

I asked, "Is everything okay?" He just repeated that I needed to have my parents call him. They must have left the hospital just minutes before my uncle passed. He wouldn't say anything more, but I wanted to hear the bad news from someone's mouth. I needed confirmation of what had just happened to me. I hung up the phone and sat quietly, waiting for my parents to come home. I knew what the feather meant; I just wasn't sure why it was happening. *Is it something normal that happens when someone passes away?* I thought. *Maybe mom and dad got one too.*

I don't remember much between that moment and the funeral. We sat toward the front of the room and my cousins (once removed, as my uncle's grandkids) were right in front of me. I could see my uncle walking around the room, listening to the stories that people were telling. He was laughing and smiling. He looked genuinely happy. I felt the sadness in the room and couldn't help but cry. This was a first for me. He was the first spirit I'd seen after knowing them in the flesh. My youngest cousin turned around and looked at me with complete confusion and innocence.

"Why are you crying?" he asked, just as William had questioned me about my fear. I didn't know how to respond; I looked at him and just kept crying. He continued, "Everything is going to be okay." There again, from his young mouth, were those sweet words that I had heard all my life. I was stunned by their impact. I knew he was right. I hadn't seen my uncle laugh that much or look that happy since he had been diagnosed with cancer. Everything truly was okay—well, everything except for the struggle of human emotions in the earthly hearts of everyone left behind.

After his funeral, I did not see my uncle much. At the time, I assumed that there were no messages to give and everyone was fine. Thinking about it now, I wonder whether he knew that no one would have believed me, had I tried to pass messages along. I will never know which it was.

When I was twenty, I wanted to share this experience with someone, anyone who would listen. I wrote my narrative as best I could. A client urged me to send it to a local Christian digest that published accounts of people's faith and other uplifting stories. My narrative was titled "On the Wings of an Angel." I sent it in to the publication and they promptly declined to publish it. Was the idea of seeing spirits and catching a feather too New Age for their publication? In retrospect, I recognize that it was very poorly written, as I had no one to give me feedback. Still, I was heartbroken. I wanted to honor my uncle. He was a hero in my eyes, and I just wanted someone who cared to recognize that. I felt it needed to be heard by someone who cared. Not only was it about my uncle and what I saw after he died, it was also about the capacity to continue to give even though you may not believe you have anything left to give. In my eyes, that ability to give is a true characteristic of a hero.

I decided to send my narrative to my aunt. I spent hours choosing paper that I thought would fit the theme. I landed on paper covered with blue skies and clouds. I thought of how the clouds must look from an angel's eyes in heaven, white and fluffy. I went to my aunt's house to deliver it by hand. She answered her door, and I just handed her the envelope and told her that I wanted her to have it. A month later, I received a short letter in the mail from her. It was a very simple thank-you note. While the words spoke gratitude, the overall tone seemed uncertain and uneasy about my experience. I wasn't sure if I should feel excited or hurt: did she believe me, think I was a sinner for using my gifts, or just not know what to think? We never spoke of it after that. Sometimes I wish I knew who she shared it with, if anyone, and what they thought. But part of me still shudders at the thought of hearing one more disbelieving comment.

Five years ago, the night before my cousin John's wedding, my husband, Brian, and I went to see a live gallery reading with Theresa Caputo, the Long Island Medium. In a venue packed with several hundred people, I was convinced she was going to deliver a message to me about my gifts. The way she described her gifts was a description of my own life. I felt like she was the answer to what I was supposed to be doing and how I could use my gifts in my life.

She started her show with a disclaimer that went something like, "Not everyone will receive direct communication from spirit tonight, but that does not mean that a message isn't for you." I ignored the disclaimer because I *knew* that I had been called by spirit to be there and that could only mean one thing: I was going to receive direct communication.

She worked her way through the gigantic crowd, walking up the aisles and delivering message after message to families dealing with great losses, unresolved family trauma, and murder. When she stopped within two rows of us, I held my breath, hoping that the next message would be for me. I was so sure that my message was coming. I was sure that I had been called to that show for a reason. She panned the crowd around us as she started to speak of a murder. *Dang it!* I thought, *this one isn't for me either!* But I still had hope that my message was coming as she walked away.

As she was wrapping up her show, she pointed to our side of the room and explained that she had a message for someone who had written a poem about heroes for someone that had passed. *Could this be my uncle?* I wondered. *It wasn't a poem, but it was about him being a hero.* I listened intently to the details. Finally, a girl in the lower section of the event center raised her hand to claim the message.

I thought about the narrative I had written about my uncle. I did believe that he was a hero, and I felt that he was around. The details about the poem didn't fit, but I struggled with giving up hope that the message was for me. My spirit guides reminded me of the disclaimer. The message may not have been for me, but I knew my uncle was close by. I asked for another sign that he was there with us. I saw nothing, I heard nothing, and I was bummed. If nothing else, John was getting married the next day, and I wanted a message from his dad to give to him.

The show ended, and as we walked out to our car, I blathered on about how that last message could have been for me but I wasn't sure. Brian just nodded and smiled. "It was an okay show," he said. He wasn't all that impressed with the show, and his skeptic side was showing.

Walking into the parking ramp, I got my message, loud and clear. Parked at the entrance of the ramp was a vehicle with my uncle's name on the plates. Next to it was an Isuzu box truck. When I was a kid, my dad and my uncle went hunting together in an old Isuzu box truck that had been converted to serve as a camper. My dad inherited that truck, and I had spent a lot of time in it as a kid. It was the perfect sign, and I knew my uncle would be at John's wedding.

The next day, at the wedding, I thought about how great it was going to be to see my uncle there. I knew, drawing from my experience at the funeral, that I would be in the minority of people that would see him. I wished that others could, but I finally understood that for most people, life didn't work that way.

My thoughts were interrupted by John's entrance. I smiled when I saw who was standing by his side: my uncle, dressed up and wearing a huge, ear-to-ear smile. My favorite smell, the smell of his tobacco pipe, wafted in my direction. It was a beautiful moment. I wanted so badly to take a picture, but I knew it wouldn't capture what I saw. I wished that everyone could have shared in that moment, in that image. I wished that I could tell everyone. But I had learned to bite my tongue and stay quiet. In my heart I knew it wouldn't have been received the way I wanted.

12

IS THIS WHAT PUBERTY IS?

*The toddler must say no in order to find out who she is.
The adolescent says no to assert who she is not.*
         —Louise J. Kaplan

For a lot of teenage girls, life revolves around crushes, getting your period, and making every word you say sound like a sexual innuendo. Oh, how I miss the days when we giggled when anyone dared say the word *pencil*. It was easier to act normal back then because everyone was awkward in their own way. My teenage years were decorated with those qualities but also tinted by regular conversations with dead people and some new, strange experiences that I wouldn't understand until years later.

When I was fourteen years old, I babysat a girl named Annie. Many people thought she was my little sister: we looked and acted alike, we were always together, and only six years separated us. One evening that October, her mom chauffeured us to a haunted house. It was an outdoor venue within a giant park, and it had several buildings, each with its own spooky theme. Outside, in the park, we could get food and play games.

We immediately stepped into a world of dead bodies, murderers, witches, skeletons, and frightening creatures that lurked patiently in the shadows until an opportunity arose for them to etch themselves into our nightmares. Slowly opening the first door, Annie started to question whether she should be in front of or behind me. With her clinging to my arm like a caterpillar on a leaf, we walked side by side into a giant meat locker. The temperature dropped drastically, and we could hear footsteps in the room with us. Instead of slabs of meat, body bags hung from the ceiling by the dozen with arms and legs flopping out. With each bag we pushed aside, the footsteps seemed to evade us. We parted the forest of body bags with no incident until the last swung out in front of us and a man with a giant butcher knife jumped into our path. Annie screamed. From that point on, she grabbed me more tightly each time someone jumped out. She was scared, but that didn't stop us.

It took us far longer than anyone else to get through that haunted house. We were passed up a few times by people who just wanted to get out of there. After that first terrifying tour, we spent hours at the different attractions, screaming and giggling. We stopped at one of the vendor booths along the way, and I let her pick out cotton candy and soda for a snack, two great things to give a child before bedtime. I teased her about being scared in the haunted house, and she huffed at me, rolled her eyes, and tried to pretend like she wasn't scared at all. We really were more like sisters than anything else.

As we walked around, eating cotton candy, we stumbled upon a tent off to the side of the park. Just outside, a sign the size of a small house read, "Tarot Readings." The whole scene reeked of old Hollywood, and I immediately thought it was a sham. The tent was the stereotypical dark blue cloth with stars and moons imprinted on the fabric. Two flaps had been tied off at the sides to create an opening, perfectly framing its inhabitant.

The tent had just enough space for her small table (showcasing her crystal ball and tarot deck) along with three chairs, one for her and two for the schmucks who stepped inside. I caught a glimpse of the woman as she stood up to straighten her skirt before sitting back down. She was beautiful and mysterious, wearing exactly the costume you'd expect: a long, dark patchwork skirt, giant hoop earrings, a colorful cloth wrapped around her long curly hair, and more bracelets than I cared to count. I was curious about her—leery, but curious. I could feel her energy pulling me in. I had to work extremely hard to convince myself that she was a whackjob, just out to get our money.

Before that moment, I had never seen Annie truly beg for anything. Now she pleaded with me as we walked toward the tent, "Please, can we go see her? Can we go see the Gypsy lady?" I told her that we didn't have enough money left to do it, but she persisted.

We gawked as we passed the tent, our mouths gaping open like fish feeding at the surface of the water. As far as I know, Annie saw nothing more than an elaborate tent with a woman inside. I saw more. Three or four spirits stood around her table, talking, as if they were guests who had been invited over for a drink. The tarot reader was listening intently to what they were saying, but all I heard was murmurs. She nodded and smiled, interjecting her comments here and there.

As we entered her field of vision, her attention broke away from the spirits and over to us. Abruptly, she sprung up from her chair and scurried to meet us at the door. She stood in the opening, framed as if she were being captured in a photograph. Her guests exchanged glances, wondering what happened. I thought she was going to give us some sales pitch to draw us in. Instead her hand shot out toward me. I jumped a little. She placed her hand on my arm, more gently than I had expected from the sudden movement.

In a tone that sounded like smoke rising up from a fire, she said, "You are very gifted and see many things that others do not see. You should come in and sit with me."

I was curious and scared at the same time. Not sure whether she was serious, I rolled my eyes and started to walk away. She stepped out of her tent and blocked my path. Fear gripped my heart, and I reached for Annie's hand.

"We don't have enough money to come in," I yelled as we scooted past her. I could see the look of disappointment on her face as we dashed away. Was it regret at losing customers or that she couldn't help me to see my gifts?

"She said come in!" Annie protested. But I projected my fears of how people thought of me onto her and tried to explain to Annie that this woman was crazy. I thought of how my friends had reacted every time I brought them into my world. I could imagine the fear that Annie would carry with her if we walked into that tent. I reiterated that the woman was crazy and just wanted our money, but in my heart, I knew that she wasn't crazy at all. If she was, so was I. I knew that I was supposed to go see her, but I couldn't bring myself to do it. I was afraid of what she might tell me. I also felt a very strong sense of protection for Annie. Every stranger-danger commercial that I had ever seen played through my head as I pulled her away.

I didn't want to understand why I was drawn to the tarot reader, and I was scared to admit that I knew I was like her. I felt I belonged there with her, in a long skirt and way too many bracelets. But admitting our gifts meant that we had to be on display, as if that costume were a label warning others of who we were and what we saw. Warning that if they spoke to us, their worlds would change and they would be forever banished to a place of fear and unexplainable messages.

Many days, I wish I had stepped into her tent. What would she have said? How would my life be different now, had I talked to her? Would I be in a completely different place? Would I be further along in my spiritual journey?

I wish I could go and talk to her now. I didn't look at her name. I didn't ask. I just ran from her. Still, I know it was meant to be this way; I am meant to learn at my own pace. It wasn't my time. These days, considering my circles of friends and the events I attend, I like to think that I have met that woman and just haven't figured it out yet. Maybe one day, when the timing is right, I will find her and we can laugh at the perfectly timed meeting that created a sense of belonging in me, even though it filled me with a sense of immense discomfort and confusion at the same time.

13

WIDE-EYED AND TIGHT-LIPPED

Few things can frustrate us more than trying to make a person someone he or she isn't; we feel crazy when we try to pretend that person is someone he or she is not.
—Melody Beattie

Belonging: a feeling that I didn't understand deeply as I was coming into my gifts. I longed to belong and yet pushed the desire away because I was afraid of how other people would see me once I was finally part of a group. My struggle to find balance between socialization and seclusion often manifested as a strong wish to leave this earth plane . . . a wish to die. As a child I had wished for death to escape the spiritual connection I had. As I grew older, I wished for death to escape the lack of human connection in my life.

I never told anyone about my thoughts when I was young. I still carried a strong sense of pride in taking care of myself and everyone around me that I had formed at an early age. Admitting my thoughts would have been weak, and as my suffocation-by-blanket attempt showed, I didn't know how to act on my thoughts anyway. As a teenager, however, I turned to hurting myself. It kept my mind off the visions I saw and the spirits who talked to me, compounding the typical teenage angst. I kept rubber bands around my wrist and snapped them when I was upset, leaving large red welts. That progressed to using the metal end of a mechanical pencil to scratch up my arms, sometimes carving words or making symbols that had meaning to me and no one else. I wore long-sleeved shirts to hide them, and I was an active kid, so any adults who did see the cuts and scratches assumed it was no big deal.

My gifts affected me more than I realized at the time. When people commented about other people being weird, it bothered me. I wondered what they said about me when I wasn't around. At the same time, my oddity never fully sunk in, and I thrived on the attention that I got for some of my gifts. I learned about acupressure and Chinese medicine while I was in junior high and high school and talked about them endlessly. At the time, I thought that talking about them was more normal than admitting the aspects of my gifts they complemented. I accepted the mocking comments that I received from fellow classmates as compliments rather than the criticisms they were intended to be. Inside I knew that they were making fun of my interests and thought I was weird, but I coped by convincing myself to believe in an alternate reality where my friends were just joking and still loved me for who I was. Sometimes it was true, but in most cases they were just making fun of me.

Like most teenagers, I had periods of time when friends turned on me, calling me weird, spreading rumors about how horrible I was, and ganging up on me. I saw others get this same treatment for long periods of time, so I told myself that it made me normal. For me, these periods of time were usually short-lived, fueled by God-knows-what, but their impact has lasted. Feeling normal didn't change my belief that something inside me was horrible and I needed to do whatever I could to sway the cosmos to make me a better person. I carried that belief with me for a very long time, and to this day, I have moments where I have to remind myself that I am good.

In junior high and high school, I was a social nomad. I was friends with the some of the popular kids, some of the so-called weirdos and freaks (whom I truly considered myself to belong to), and anyone else who would be my friend. But I didn't date anyone. Most of my friends were starting to date, and I was almost always the third or fifth wheel. In seventh grade, one of my friends—one of the popular boys—said something hinting that he liked me in front of a group of guys. One of them said, "Why would you say that to that freak? She is so weird." Even though he said it right in front of me, it didn't hurt my feelings. Acting cocky for a girl who had never had a boyfriend, I turned the razzing that I received for being weird into a (slightly delusional) belief that people had crushes on me but were too afraid of my *weird* label to tell anyone. Besides, I knew in my heart that his statement was truth: I had weird secrets that no one could ever imagine.

I knew that one boy's grandma had just passed away and he was struggling with it. I knew that various teachers were carrying around guilt because they hadn't gotten to say goodbye to loved ones who had passed. Other teachers were struggling in their marriages or with their own mental health. Needless to say, I knew way too much for a teenager. In my mind, that made me weird.

When I was a senior in high school, my friends convinced me to join an instant messaging community online. I met a guy there who took an interest in me. It was among my first experiences with a guy who talked to me as if he loved me and was truly interested in getting to know me. In less than a year, I learned a lot of what *not* to do from him. He lived in another state but came to visit me. Our relationship is where I learned what true mental health issues look like. I thought of the relationship as loving at first, but it was really filled with control issues, violence, and immense trauma.

Each day he was in my home, my spirit guides asked me to take a deeper look at who he was and who I was. I sat silent while they pounded me with very real, very honest questions: "Is this the person that he said he was? Do you trust him? Why do you think you need him?" They asked me to examine every aspect of the relationship. I needed to feel like I belonged with someone. I needed to feel like I was loveable and good. I needed someone to give me attention. But the more my spirit guides questioned me, the more I realized that I did not like the way he treated me or my family or my friends. I did not like the person that he was. Most of all, I started to realize that I didn't *need* anyone. What I needed was to accept myself, love myself, and give myself attention. His presence in my life allowed me to begin healing. It also allowed me to begin finding strength to be the person that I was put on this earth to be. Unfortunately, it took his abuse and obsessive behavior for me to start to recognize this.

Shortly after his departure from Minnesota, I started weighing my post–high school career options and making decisions about my future. I chose to enroll in a yearlong massage therapy program at a local vocational university and also began an eighteen-month relationship. Both changed my life, but only one ended free from heartbreak. Just two month after graduating from the massage therapy program, my relationship ended and I found myself wallowing in old beliefs again. I convinced myself that I was a horrible and unlovable person, and no one would care if I were gone. I went into a tailspin trying to deal with my emotions. My cutting and self-harm habits intensified.

Two months later, my parents went out of town for the weekend, leaving me home alone. I sat in my room crying, holding a large kitchen knife and trying to decide if I was really going to slit my wrists. As I thought about it, everything else went quiet. My head was so full of thoughts of suicide that I could only vaguely hear the constant chatter of the spirits around me, urging me to stop. William and Jay sat on the edge of my bed: their mouths moved and their faces pleaded with me, but I heard nothing. Two women, who I assumed were my spirit guides, stood on either side of my bed, speaking words I could not understand. Their eyes were full of sorrow and compassion. I heard no words, but the graceful movement of their mouths soothed my nerves.

For the first time in my life, a twisted but peaceful silence fell around me.

I began to think about how I would be found and how horrible it would be for my family. I must have put that knife up to my skin twenty-five times before I decided to cut myself. At the last minute I flipped my wrist over and cut the top of my left forearm rather than my wrist. I was surprised at how easily the knife cut my skin and how little it hurt. Then I was horrified that I did it. It was so easy. I was scared that I would do it again and really kill myself.

The chatter came back. The four spirits in my room had multiplied, and the peaceful murmur in the background was now a roar of emotion. A barrage of comments and questions flooded my ears so quickly that I couldn't place whose mouth they were coming from. Concern: "Jenni, please stop!" Frustration: "It is not your time!" Compassion: "Dear child, you are loved more than you can imagine." And confusion: "Why did you do that?" The last words were from William's mouth. He pleaded with me, "Please, please, don't do it again!" I could see that he was afraid. My room was full of people who didn't understand what I had just done, and to top it off, I was now mad at myself for being so weak. I don't know if I thought I was weak because I didn't cut my wrist or because I'd cut myself at all.

With the knife in my left hand and my right hand gripped tightly over the two-inch gash on my arm, I ran upstairs to the bathroom. Although I was still bleeding, I washed the knife in the shallow sink. Then I ran to the kitchen and wrapped my arm in a tight cast of wet paper towels to make the bleeding stop. It must have looked like I was trying to cover up a murder: running through the house, wielding a knife, trying to contain the blood, wash up the crime scene, and dispose of the bloody weapon.

Why are you so stupid? I thought. *Why did you do that?* Finally I curled up on the counter in the bathroom, shaking. I didn't want to be alone in my house; I didn't trust myself anymore.

I certainly didn't trust my thoughts to lead me in the right direction. Confused and scared to admit what I had done, I went straight back to the c-word. I didn't want anyone to think I was crazy. Thank goodness I had one person who wouldn't judge me, no matter what. I called Sarah. She told me to come over and let myself in.

I put the knife back in the drawer in the kitchen and drove over to her house. It was 12:30 in the morning. She was in bed, so as she'd instructed, I let myself in and went to her room. Still half asleep, she looked at my arm and calmly said, "I've seen much worse." I am pretty sure she was trying to reassure me, but those were not the words I felt I needed to hear in that moment. However, I clung to them in order to keep my mind off the horrible thing that I'd just done. Shame was taking root in my body.

I stayed with her until morning and then went back home. I felt depressed and ashamed of myself, but confident that I wouldn't cut myself again. My temporary bandage did its job. The wound stopped bleeding and started to heal, but there was no hiding it. I sat around feeling sorry for myself, or angry, or maybe both. What would I tell my parents when they saw my arm? The tears started. My parents would be devastated to know that I was contemplating suicide. With the thought of their disappointment in my head, I sat in the bathroom and sobbed for hours.

When my parents returned, I was still in the bathroom, huddled in a fetal position on the counter. They asked me what was wrong, and I told them that I had cut myself. My dad looked shocked, like he didn't know what to do. My mom took my hand and led me to my room. Time passed slowly as we talked. I lay on my stomach, arms stretched out above my head on my bed, sobbing into my pillow. Mom sat next to my bed, rubbing my back and asking questions.

"Do we need to bring you in to the hospital?" she finally asked. I told her that I didn't know, still afraid that they would label me *crazy*. As I finished my sentence, a single white feather fell from the ceiling and landed directly in the palm of my right hand. My heart raced, my tears stopped, and my mind was completely clear.

I looked at my mom and said, "Yes, I think I need to go into the hospital."

Puzzled, my mom asked about the feather, "Where did that come from?"

I simply replied, "They always fall when something in my life ends." I knew that something was about to change, and if I went to the hospital it would somehow end my suffering.

My parents took me to St. Joseph's Hospital in St. Paul. I was informed that I would be placed on a seventy-two-hour hold because I had admitted myself for mental health reasons. They were very nice about it, and I even received a new wardrobe, including a fabulous pair of slipper socks and shoo-ins for an ugly pajama contest. My pants were a dim grey with mauve and teal pinstripes. The shirt echoed the color in a diamond print instead. The outfit was completed with my low-cut, black combat boots. It was pretty darn comfortable.

They transferred me to the mental health department at a different hospital, and because I had already been admitted I had to ride in an ambulance. I was excited for the new experience, and they even let me push buttons on the way!

When I arrived at the second hospital, I entered the mental health ward through a set of locked doors. The doctors and nurses flitted in and out of the doors so often that if you stood there for a split second you could memorize the passcode and let yourself back out. I didn't care enough to try it, but I hoped that their patient information security was better than their ability to hide that code from the patients it was meant to keep in.

As I signed in, the nurse took away anything with a cord or a point, sharp or dull; anything that could be used as a shank or a noose. It scared me to know that I wasn't allowed to have a Walkman, pens or pencils, a belt, shoelaces, or headphones because they suspected that I might try to kill myself. For the first time since I was a child, I would have to ask to use my Walkman or a pencil. The rest of my belongings were brought to my room. I was supposed to be bunking with another woman, but I never had the opportunity to meet her. The day I was admitted, another patient told me that my roommate had tried to cut herself and had been put in another room for closer observation. Our room was right outside the nurse's station; I wondered how observation could get any closer than that.

Within a few hours a psychologist came to see me. He asked standard questions: Had I ever been on medication? Was I feeling suicidal? How often did I want to hurt myself? Afterward, he gave me a new medication that I really didn't want to take. I had been on an antidepressant once before and hated the way that it made me feel. And I certainly didn't want to take medication that they gave to people who were in the hospital because they needed medication. Medication meant I was one more step closer to being labeled. I was starting to rethink my decision to come to the hospital.

After my drug meeting, the doctors and nurses left me to my own devices. I was free to wander the cage and talk to the other inmates. I, of course, gravitated to the patients who made the most noise, laughed often, and talked to the most people. I joined up with several guys, slightly older than me, who were playing cards, making phone calls, and joking with the other patients. These were my new friends for the next seventy-two hours. The next morning another gal, also close to my age, joined us as well. Every break that we got from group meetings and appointments with the doctors, we met in the middle of the common area to play cards. At meals we sat together. It felt like high school, except for the fact that we weren't allowed to leave and were required to take drugs.

We joked that we sat at the cool kids' table. All of us were hyperaware that we had issues—some more severe than others—but we also knew that our oddities were part of our uniqueness. When you are sitting in a psychiatric ward, it is hard not to compare yourself to the other patients. Some of the people there could barely communicate because their mental health was so bad. At our table, we could at least say, "Life sucks right now, but overall, it isn't so bad." We knew that we needed to be there at that time, but jokes about escaping from the "nuthouse" dropped at least every twenty minutes. It was an uncomfortable coping mechanism for those of us who didn't want to admit that we needed to be there or that we were afraid of the label we would get for being there. But being in community with others like me alleviated some of my fear.

As much fun as we tried to have, it wasn't a great place to be. There was a constant, dull mumbling from patients down the hall, bells and chimes from the room alarms, and occasional high-pitched squawking from someone who didn't want to take their meds, couldn't remember where they were, or just wanted to go home. Fights broke out daily, which amped up the noise level. They were always short, more lip action than physical action: I only saw one punch thrown, and to be honest, I wouldn't have been worried about it if it had been directed at me.

One man flailed a limp arm at another, who deflected the blow with no visible effort, turned his back, scoffed, rolled his eyes, and walked away. I got the feeling that this rodeo was fairly routine for them.

We were each assigned a list of daily tasks, such as weighing ourselves, taking our blood pressure, signing up for group sessions, and filling out activity sheets. I was informed that because of the "nature of my visit," two group sessions a day were required as well as an individual goal-setting class and a creative activity.

I was, of course, overjoyed at the prospect of sharing my feelings and tears with complete strangers. I thought, *I would rather take my meds than sit in one of these group classes, and I would rather lick a razor than take my meds.*

My first group session took place in a room barely big enough to fit the four tables that were set up for the fourteen attendees. I was certain that they did this on purpose, so no one flew the coop. I sat as close to the door as I could, just in case I wanted to get the heck out of there. I would only have to dive over three people to escape.

The tables were arranged in a square so we could look at each other while we spoke. Most people pretended to understand as everyone cried about whatever was bugging them that day. Half of what was said was so unintelligible that even though I was listening, I couldn't make sense of the sobbing. It was near impossible to respond with encouragement when I didn't know what someone said. Thank goodness our group leader spoke the language of tears. She always had an encouraging word to share, and it usually made sense.

I am a terrible crier. It's a miracle if anyone can understand anything I say when I cry. My face contorts until it resembles a suckerfish that has been bludgeoned with a carp. Snotty ooze drips from my nose, my face turns red, and my eyes swell up. I am pretty sure that no one had any idea what I was saying for my first three minutes of sobbing, and I don't think anyone was really listening to me anyway. The group was nice to me, though, and that counts for something: I didn't try to escape.

After my first group experience, I went back to my room and went to bed. I thought groups were a pointless waste of time that weren't good for anything other than making me cry. When I woke up, it was time for another group session. Yay!

You could hear sighs of relief as we walked into the room for the next session. The room was about ten times the size of the last room. I could breathe without someone smelling my breath and cry without splattering someone with tears. It was set up like a classroom. The topic: Coping through Thoughts of Suicide.

I needed this discussion, but I secretly wished for a subtitle: What to Do When You See Dead People, or maybe, What to Say When Spirits Talk to You. Still, that group session gave me many of the tools that I still use to control my responses to unhealthy thought patterns and live with my gifts. Looking back, I still think it's funny. *Who knew going to a mental hospital could teach me coping skills and alleviate some of my fears?*

My experiences in the mental health ward were eye-opening, not just because of what I learned, but also because of the people that I met. I truly enjoyed all the people there with me. They were honest about who they were—well, more honest than most are outside the hospital. They didn't hide their flaws, and most accepted everything as it was. It was the least judgmental social setting I had ever been in.

Several of the people had been there a while or came back often enough that everyone knew them, patients and staff alike. One of the men coped with his mental disorders by startling the nurses. It was obnoxious, but it was all he could do to make his life more fun and mentally manageable. It also gave the rest of us something to take our minds off our problems, and it taught me a deeper lesson about mindset. On my first day, one of the guys pulled me aside at shift change, saying, "Watch this: it's *hilarious!*"

The nurses' shifts changed at the same time every day, and he used this to his advantage. As the nurses came down the long hallway, he would stand by the door and wait. We could hear the beep of each number on the keypad. *Beep . . . beep . . . beep . . .* wait for it . . . just one more number . . . *beep,* and *click!*

As the door swung open and the nurse started to slip in, he rushed the door, spinning and turning as if he were carrying a football into the end zone on a last-ditch effort to win the Super Bowl. The startled nurse would slam the door shut and peer through the small window in the door, head shaking in disapproval, as he stood bent over in the hallway, grasping at his belly as it undulated with laughter.

I laughed harder than I had in years. Even the nurses laughed; I think they understood that it was his way of coping, though they couldn't take the chance that he would actually get out. He always stopped at least five feet from the door and made sure to apologize to the nurses when they finally came in. In an odd way, I admired him. He didn't seem to care what anyone thought of him, and he remained positive even though his life wasn't what he wanted it to be. He had been in the mental hospital on and off for over ten years with a diagnosis of bipolar disorder and schizophrenia. Rather than feeling sorry for himself, he embraced the fact that the hospital would be there as often as he needed it. He explained to me that when he had episodes he couldn't control himself. Medication would only work for so long before they had to change it again, and yet he remained positive.

That was something that I couldn't say for myself. My positivity had been waning for a while. On my first day he told me, "Don't get down about being here. It isn't that bad. We all walk through shit sometimes." He did what he wanted, no matter what anyone said. He was the one who had to live in his head; no one could fix that for him, so he did what he had to do to enjoy his "crazy" life. I wished that I could learn to just be me, spirits and all, without fearing what other people thought. If he could do it, maybe I could too.

After watching the three o'clock door show, I rushed off to my individual goal-setting session. I had almost forgotten that I had places to be. As I walked into the small classroom, I was handed a packet of forms to fill out. Each asked different questions about what I would like to accomplish, how it would help me, what I needed to be successful, and how I thought I could accomplish these things. These questions were easy. None of them seemed to be about my emotions.

My recent graduation from the massage program was one of the few things I was excited about. I laid out my love of massage therapy and penned in my goal to start my own massage company. I scribbled in as much detail as I could muster. For the rest of the evening, I dreamed about what my business would look like, who my clients would be, how happy I would be, and most of all, who I could help. This goal gave me something to live for: helping other people. I knew it would help me as much as it did others.

In my last twenty-four hours at the hospital, I got to know a very sweet gentleman in his eighties. He gave up his seat for the ladies in the room whenever possible, and he opened doors for us, even when we didn't see the door. He'd had a rough life that revolved around severe childhood abuse. Now he walked the halls, talking to people that only he could see. He told me about the people who talked to him. Many of them had been with him since he was a child.

His parents beat him for talking to himself and told him, from a young age, that he was crazy. After hearing it over and over again, he started to believe it. His voice quivered as he said, "After you start to believe you're crazy, it gets worse. It comes true." That scared me because he and I were a lot alike; there were days when I believed wholeheartedly that I was 110 percent insane.

He explained to me that the people he talked to tried to stuck up for him, but his parents couldn't see or hear them. These friends would console him when his parents got angry and tell him how to take care of his wounds so he wouldn't get sick.

His emotions got the best of him as he relived the time they stopped talking to him so he wouldn't get in trouble anymore: "It was a far worse punishment than any beating I ever got." Only a child at the time, he thought his friends had abandoned him and didn't like him anymore. He was devastated. I breathed in sharply as he described the worst part: even when he stopped talking to his invisible friends, the beatings from his parents didn't stop. They found new reasons to beat him. He ate too slow, he ate too fast, he didn't answer their questions fast enough or in the correct way. Thankfully, after that realization, his friends came back. I closed my eyes, feeling his pain as I thought about the times when William had disappeared for days or months. I thought about how scared I was without him there with me. I knew that this amazing man and I shared something.

There were others at the hospital who talked to people that no one else saw; most were medicated for it. That was a problem for me. Sometimes I could see the same people they did. They were very real, but they were spirits, not figments of someone's imagination. I learned very quickly not to tell the nurses that I saw them too.

Those experiences broke something inside me that I will never be able to fix. Knowing some of these people were being treated for mental illness because they had a gift no one understood shattered my dream of being "normal." I didn't know what to do. So I protected myself. I didn't tell a soul in that place what I saw. I sat in my room and repeated to myself every day, "I am not that bad, I am not that bad, I am not that bad . . . I know that what I see is real." I knew my issues; I knew what I needed to learn, and because the doctors all thought I was just "having a rough go" with a bout of depression, my stay ended after those seventy-two long and eventful hours.

My experiences in the hospital taught me about self-acceptance. I learned to manage my suicidal thoughts. They didn't go away, but I no longer acted on them. When I started to accept myself, my flaws and my abilities, I found that my depression had more to do with feeling like I was an outcast than my ability to see spirits. Would I still feel like an outcast if I didn't have these gifts? Who knows? It's possible that there would be other reasons to feel this way. My biggest need was to learn to accept my gifts fully and let people get to know all of me. I also needed to find a group of people who understood and accepted me. Once I saw how the people at the hospital accepted each other, I knew it was possible.

I left the hospital that day, joyful that I could leave, but with an extremely heavy heart. Knowing that people who could see what I saw had to stay there because they weren't lucky enough to avoid the "crazy" label made me cringe. I regret that I never fessed up to them. My escape felt unfair. If they had to be there, then maybe I was supposed to be there too, not because any of us needed to be there, but because they had already done their time and I felt like I was bailing on them. Maybe I was supposed to help them understand their gifts. Maybe I had a bigger purpose to fulfill by being there. Then again, maybe I was supposed to be there to see what not to do, who not to tell. Or maybe it was just an experience that I was meant to have so I could see the difference between mental health needs and spirituality. No matter how I spin it, I still wonder if I could have helped some of those people or if, on some level, I did help them like they helped me. If not, I hope that by educating people, I can help create a space for people to be free of that place as well as that stigma.

14

NOT EVERY ROSE HAS ITS THORNS

*What's in a name? That which we call a rose
by any other name would smell as sweet.*
—William Shakespeare,
Romeo and Juliet

While I was in the hospital, I finalized my plans to start my massage business. After I was released, digging in to the details was the best way to keep my mind occupied. Work became my main coping mechanism. At nineteen, when I opened my mobile massage clinic, I became a workaholic.

As I stepped out in the business world and opened myself up to helping others lessen the stress of their lives, I started getting more intentional and structured communications from spirits. They started to seek me out to give messages to my clients. Unfortunately, I ignored most of them when they stepped forward. I wasn't ready yet. I still thought people would think I was crazy, and I feared that my messages would be horribly inaccurate—or, worse yet, completely true for people who weren't ready to hear them. Long story short, I was afraid that I was making stuff up and equally afraid that I was truly a medium. I wasn't sure I wanted to participate in either of those narratives just yet. I didn't fully trust myself or the messages I was receiving.

Over the years, I have found out that I am not the only one to go through that phase. Whether you are a medium or a marine biologist, it is part of learning self-acceptance and trust. It is also a huge lesson in letting go of the fear that others will judge you, one that, to this day, I still have to work on.

While I struggled to decide if I would share the messages coming through, my intuition kicked up a notch. I started to see things about people that I hadn't seen before, or at least I didn't recognize. I could feel what people were feeling, and I could see what was happening inside their body on a whole new level. I was confused. On one hand, I felt as if I had to keep hiding my gifts. On the other hand, I knew that if I were supposed to hide them, I would not be receiving so much information. I had a sense that after all the years I had spent censoring myself, I was now being asked to share everything in detail with my clients. I was already afraid of being called a liar and rejected. Now I feared that I would lose my ability to pay my bills, too! Just what I needed: a whole new level of fear.

The more I tried to hide my gifts and ignore the spirits who came to me during sessions, the more they started bothering me at night. They would poke at me while I slept, talk louder and louder until I couldn't ignore them anymore, or follow me around day after day, repeating their messages like a broken record. At that time, I didn't know that I could tell them to stop, and I was too afraid to give the messages to my clients. I felt like I was failing everyone, especially the spirits, since my clients had no idea that I was holding back. One day, that all changed for me.

During a massage session with a new client, the spirit of an older woman stepped forward to give a message to me. The glare of white light off of her was blinding. I couldn't see her, but I could *feel* everything about her. Like smelling chocolate-chip cookies so strongly that you can taste them, I sensed her so strongly that I could see every movement she made in my mind. She was a sweet old woman, like a character from *Leave It to Beaver* or *The Andy Griffith Show*: the kind of woman who wore a frilly apron, had her hair done just right, always had dinner on the table when her family got home, and baked everyone's favorite cookies once a week. She emanated nothing but love, unconditional love. She leaned over my client and kissed him on the forehead, and her light shone throughout his body. She put her hand on his chest, and I could see the white light penetrate his heart. She was sharing her love with him.

I took a deep breath and noticed the scent of fresh-cut roses filling the room. It was immediately followed by the scent of homemade chocolate-chip cookies. Her energy smiled at me. Slowly, her light faded and she disappeared. For the rest of the session I debated how to tell my client what had just happened. There was no message to speak of, only the love of a grandmother who wanted her grandson to know she was there. I knew in my heart that he needed to know and that I had to tell him. But how? He was a brand-new client.

At the end of all of my sessions I share with my clients anything that I found in the body to help them with their healing process. A visit from a spirit was uncharted territory for me, and I was scared of what was about to happen. Even so, I finished up the session and stepped out to wash my hands while my client got up. When I came back into the room, I started explaining the muscles I had found that were tight and stretches he could do to ease them. Then it happened.

I blurted out, "Did you have a grandma named Rose?" The look on his face and the size of his eyes told me that he did, so I just kept talking as fast as I could. The words spilled from my mouth. If I didn't stop, maybe he couldn't think I was crazy. "She stepped forward today so that you knew she was with you. Did you used to bake chocolate-chip cookies with her?"

Still shocked, he asked, "How did you know that?" I explained as much as I knew how to explain but still didn't really understand myself.

We talked for a long time that day. My client was ecstatic. I was ecstatic, too. It felt good to finally share my gifts with someone. It felt even better to share my gifts with someone who accepted them as truth and didn't call me crazy. That was the day that I decided to start sharing my truth with other people. Very carefully, and with great hesitation, I started integrating my spiritual gifts into sessions.

I still have days when I struggle with sharing information with people. Sometimes a message comes through that makes no sense at all—to me. When I share those messages, my client usually cries and explains the meaning to me. However, there are always moments when my client looks at me like I am nuts or tells me they have no clue what I am talking about. My heart still breaks when it happens. The saving grace, though, is that they almost always come back later to tell me that they figured out what it meant. Those days make it worthwhile, and the messages that change lives open my heart to a new kind of joy that I cannot even explain.

15

HEART OF THE PROBLEM

Your heart serves as the compass for your actions, guiding you to do the right thing when your soul becomes lost.
—Anthony William,
Medical Medium

I began to learn self-acceptance during my hospital stay and continued to process it as I started delivering messages to my clients. However, I still struggled with accepting many aspects of myself. I was very good at compartmentalizing my gifts, accepting some and leaving others to linger in the back of my mind like an unexpected guest at a cocktail party. One of the gifts that I have struggled to accept (or even admit aloud) is my ability to see disease and dysfunction within the structures of the body. I am a medical medium. Medical mediums often feel when something is wrong before it is actually diagnosed by the Western medical community. As a massage therapist, I cannot and do not claim to treat, diagnose, or cure any disease, and for that reason, I have always been very careful about the comments I make to clients about what I am feeling in the body. I am not a doctor, and I would hate to lead someone down the wrong path of treatment.

Since I was eleven years old, I can remember touching people and thinking about what diseases might be lingering in their bodies. I could hear things growing inside them. I could see the tissues tearing from injury, the heart beating irregularly, the blackness in the lungs from too much smoking, the deterioration of the liver from too much alcohol, the pain from depression . . . I could see and feel all of it. I used to pretend I had an overactive imagination. That, somehow, the things I saw came from really detailed episodes of *The Magic School Bus*. This gift seemed far stranger than my ability to see and talk to dead people.

When I started in massage school, my ability to hear the body was an issue. My instructors worked very hard to teach proper body mechanics while we worked on clients. One instructor, Bryan, would say, "Jenn, you are tilting your head again and you shouldn't kneel down when you work." I always responded the same whiny way: "But I can hear the body better this way." He would then cock his head to one side, squint, and squeak out a noise that I can only imagine meant, "Huh?" He never gave up on me, though. He reminded me to stand up at least six times a day and would lightly touch the side of my head as he passed by to remind me that I was tilting my head. One day he went so far as to put tape on my neck so it would pull at my skin when I tilted my head. It was a good reminder, but I still tilt my head and kneel down when I work. That posture is the culprit behind my spinal misalignments and need for regular chiropractic visits. At least I think about it when I do it now!

He was a phenomenal teacher and taught me more than I could have ever imagined in the short time that we had with him as a teacher. To this day, I go over my notes from his class and look at his posts online to double-check his opinion on things. I just wish he and everyone else could have heard what I heard in class.

The other thing my instructors loved about me was my propensity to tell people that they should go to the doctor to check out health concerns. I never diagnosed anything, and I never claimed to know why I was telling people to go get them checked. I would simply tell them that with the symptoms that they were reporting, it would be wise to follow up with a doctor. I almost always knew why I was telling them, but I couldn't explain it without fearing that I would sound crazy or get onto shaky legal ground. If an instructor heard me, I'd get the usual lecture: "You need to be careful not to cross the line . . ."

After I got out of school, those words became my mantra. I was extremely careful about what I said, but there were times when I just *had* to tell my clients to get checked out. In my head, the consequences would be far greater if they didn't.

Luckily, most of my clients didn't argue with my "feelings." They just trusted my intuition and, even without a real reason to go, made appointments. Three instances I will never forget.

The first was a friend and business colleague, Charlene. From the day I met her at a networking meeting, I trusted her more than I trusted most people. Her honesty showed that she cared about me. She was my first business coach but became a friend as well. We saw each other weekly and talked about aspects of my business that I needed to work on as well as aspects that I excelled in. She had an amazing gift of seeing every aspect of a person. She knew that I was intuitive before I shared it with the world; she saw how deep my gifts ran and how they permeated everything I did in business. She would joke, "When are you coming over to work your frou-frou magic on me?" I would laugh, and we would set up a time for a massage. I knew that she was making it a joke because neither of us knew what to call it.

After I had worked with her for a while, I started to notice that the energy in her head was changing. It was building up like a volcano inside her skull about to erupt. Something was wrong. There was a pressure present that shouldn't have been, and not being a doctor, I had no idea what it was. I told her for months that I was worried that something was going on in her head, in the only way that I knew how. "You have too much energy building up in your head. It doesn't feel right. Maybe you should get it checked out." She laughed it off a few times as stress or too much work on her mind. Being young and inexperienced, I finally agreed and assumed that she was right. I convinced myself that it was her body and she knew it better than I did. I really didn't have a track record yet as a medical medium, so after the same conversation month after month, I let it go.

The pressure remained in her head, at times increasing in intensity, and my concern never left. I broached the subject one last time, offering up a half-joking, "I'm worried your head is going to explode." She laughed it off once again, and I agreed to let it go, again. Shortly after that conversation, I was filling out paperwork and going over my business plan at my desk when a beautiful white feather fell from the ceiling. Slowly and peacefully, it tumbled down into the palm of my right hand. I started to panic. Something in my life or someone's life had just come to a very abrupt end. I ran through the imaginary file in my brain, checking to see who was ill. I listed off all of my clients, family members, and friends of a certain age and silently ran through their medical history. No one came to mind. I went to sleep that night in a cold sweat, waiting for a phone call.

It came the next morning. I could barely understand the words spoken on the other end between the sobs and the sniffling. It was Chris, another friend and business colleague. He was sobbing uncontrollably. I didn't know what was happening. I had never heard him cry before, and his sobs created a distressing feeling in my body.

At last I understood: our friend Charlene had passed away from a brain aneurysm. Our conversation ended as it started, in unintelligible sobs. I sat in shock for what felt like an eternity, wishing that I had pushed harder for her to go to the doctor and blaming myself for her death. Soon after, I spoke to her partner, Lana. The words that came from her mouth will be forever etched in my brain, "Did you know it was an aneurysm? Why didn't you tell her?" Her tone felt like blame to me, and even thirteen years later, the tone still stings. What if I had pushed a little harder or laughed about Charlene's stress levels a little bit less? An eerie chill crosses my body when I think about the joke I made when I approached the subject the last time. In the end, I know that it wouldn't have changed the outcome. Charlene wouldn't have been any less stubborn about going to the doctor, and even if she had, they couldn't have fixed the problem.

I am blessed that I can still talk to her after her passing; she comes to visit me fairly often. She comments on my business choices, reminds me of things that we talked about years ago, and assures me that no matter how hard I could have pushed, nothing would have changed what happened. Right after her passing, she used to say, "The only thing that would have changed is the amount of guilt you feel now." Without her assurance, I don't know that I could have gotten through the guilt.

After that experience, I started looking for legitimate ways to tell clients about my concerns without diagnosing anything and remaining on the Eastern medical side of the line. I was lucky enough to have an acupuncturist who believed in me and my gifts enough to become my unofficial mentor. Estelle was an amazingly feisty woman, and her blunt New Yorker honesty helped shape the person and practitioner that I am today. At times her honesty was harsh, but I loved and appreciated it nonetheless. She taught acupuncture at the local college and played an important part in shaping the program there. While some of her students thought she was too hard on them, I have a feeling that she might have set high standards to make students work for their success. Every time I went to see her she asked, "When are you going to enroll in acupuncture courses?"

I met her when she was eighty-two and still a force to be reckoned with. She didn't become an acupuncturist until she was in her fifties, and for some reason that made her even more of an inspiration to me. That, and the fact that she believed in me. She believed so deeply that I had what it takes to be an acupuncturist that she gave me her old acupuncture charts and started a list of books I would need to enroll in the program at the college. I often think, *Maybe when I am in my fifties I will go back to school for acupuncture. Then I can be like Estelle.* Like Charlene, she comes to visit me on a regular basis, mostly to encourage me to keep learning and harass me about going back to school.

She used to talk to me about the stagnation of chi (life energy) in my body, in each organ, and describe the meridians in the body. We talked about how the body spoke to us and how, if you listen closely, we could hear what it says. She was the first person I knew who completely understood what I was hearing. From listening to her, I learned how to talk to my clients about what I was sensing and weave my words carefully to caution people about potential health concerns. I learned to spin a web of information, starting with the muscle tension patterns and, strand by strand, adding more information about how those areas of tension affect them emotionally and physically, how the points along the meridians correlate to other areas of the body, and how energy shifts can affect the body's function. It is an art that I am not sure I could have learned on my own.

Estelle passed away in 2008. At the time, I hadn't seen her for a few years, and I regret it deeply. I was ashamed that I didn't have the financial stability to get regular acupuncture treatments anymore. She called me several times to check in and ask if I wanted to work with her as a massage therapist at her clinic. I was too stubborn and ashamed of my perceived shortcomings to call her back. It breaks my heart to think that I was too worried about money to realize she was still trying to mentor me. I know that I could have learned a lot more from her while she was on this earth, but thankfully, I continue to learn from her even now that she is gone.

At times, I can hear her voice ask me during a session, "What meridian is that?" I laugh as she asks me when I am going back to school for acupuncture. I tell her that I am following in her footsteps, and once I turn fifty, I will look into it. She quietly reminds me of the verbal quizzes she gave me while I lay on the acupuncture table in her office. She even followed me through a bookstore once to point out a book that I needed to purchase. It wasn't on the list of required reading for college, but she needed to add it anyway. She is just as feisty now as she was while she walked this earth, and I am forever grateful that she is still committed to being my mentor.

Years after Charlene and Estelle passed away, a client slunk painfully into my office. In years of weekly appointments, I had never seen such anguish on her face as I saw that day. I heard her body tell me that she had something growing inside of her spleen. I got scared. I was afraid to tell her but afraid not to tell her at the same time. I didn't want to have the same experience with her as I did with Charlene.

I felt like a confused five-year-old soccer player on the losing team, running back and forth on the field, not sure which goal was mine to shoot at. When I finally got the chance to kick the ball, I was so afraid that I was going to kick it into the wrong goal that I just gave the ball to someone else.

I didn't want to be wrong *or* right about my client's health. I didn't want to scare her for no reason, and I certainly didn't want to come across as diagnosing her medical condition. My Trapper Keeper brain flipped back through its pages to reveal the information that Estelle had taught me. I began to explain that I was feeling a change in the energy flow in points relating to the spleen. "I think it would be wise to get it checked out by a doctor," I concluded. She promised me that she would call her doctor when she got home.

The following week she came in for her appointment and the look on her face was a jumble of emotions. Fear, concern, and gratitude marked her face instead of pain. I was confused. I feared the words that were about to spill from her mouth. Part of me wanted to hide so I didn't have to hear the news I knew she was going to share. She grabbed me as soon as she walked in and gave me a hug that could crush cinder block. Still hugging me, she started to weep as she recounted the past week. After she'd left her previous appointment with me, she had called her doctor. I am not sure what she said to him, but he got her into the office right away.

Cancer was filling her spleen and was spreading rapidly throughout her lymphatic system. The prognosis was not good, and they only gave her a few months to live. As her hug let up, she looked me in the eyes and, with the deepest gratitude, told me that I had just given her a chance to do all the things she wouldn't have done, had she not known about her cancer. She was certain that, had I not encouraged her to go in, they would never have found it before she was gone. I was humbled by the confidence in her statement and yet incredibly sad to be part of her cancer story. She started to travel immediately, checking items off her bucket list. Unfortunately, I saw her only two more times. Even before that experience, she had called me her angel of mercy. She said that God sent me to her to provide relief to her pain. After her diagnosis, I call her my blessing in disguise.

Without her expression of gratitude, I might not have continued to tell my clients what I saw and felt. I did not see it as a gift until I saw how thankful she was. Without my blessing in disguise, this gift would have become the curse I refused to talk about. She was not the only one of my clients to call me an angel over the years. In fact, the majority of my clients over the age of sixty called me one form of angel or another. I was deemed to be the angel of mercy, the healing angel, the earth angel, and the angel of peace. I enjoyed my titles but passed them off as typical nicknames, passed out on a whim. After all, my older clients also called me "my little parsnip" and "my sweet rutabaga." But I was more than happy to carry all of these titles if it meant I got to help people.

One problem I saw in many clients was an irregular heartbeat. I worked with an older population of clients, and a large number of them had heart concerns already diagnosed. I started to become accustomed to the feeling of a rubber glove surrounding the heart. The stifled sound of the heartbeat, the irregular rhythm, the muted blood flow, and low energy going to and from the heart seemed commonplace.

I expected to feel the rubber glove from time to time, but the day I felt a thick, wet towel around someone's heart, I froze. The sensation was so shocking to me that I almost gasped when I felt it. My client didn't have diagnosed heart concerns. She was fairly healthy, and I was ill prepared for this discovery. I started to ready myself for the conversation after her session but was having a hard time coming up with the words to express how concerned I was about her heart.

After she got up off the table and was dressed, I explained that the energy around her heart was stagnant. She asked a few questions, and I just blurted out, "You NEED to go to the doctor. I feel like something is wrong with your heart." I was so worried about what I felt that I could not control the words that burst out of my mouth like a meteor shooting across the sky, quick but unmistakable. By the time I left her house, she already had plans to call her doctor. Thank goodness she did, because the next day they ended up putting in a pacemaker. The fact that her doctors found this issue before she had a heart attack was one more blessing.

I question daily why I was given this specific means of insight. How am I able to feel the things I do, and why can I hear things as they grow and change in the body when other people can't? Sometimes I even question if there is a different name for my gift. The term *medical medium* fills me with intense discomfort. If I am a medical medium, why don't I always see what is happening? Why can't I see everyone's cancer? Diabetes, MS, lupus, Alzheimer's? I have found that there is no guarantee the information is there for me, just like there is no guarantee that a spirit will step forward when I ask them to. At times I hear nothing but the movement of the muscles. Other times, I feel the tears in the tissue, the strains in each muscle fiber, and the tension that creates people's pain but hear nothing about organs or disease within the body. Some days I feel like there must be a little kid inside my head, plugging my ears and screaming, "Lalalalalalala!" to block out the other information.

I will likely never know why I can feel some things and not others. For now, I will choose to accept the information that I receive as one more blessing and trust that the other information wouldn't have helped the person even if I could have shared it.

16

A DEMON, A SKEPTIC, AND A MEDIUM WALK INTO MY BEDROOM

Believe in yourself! Have faith in your abilities!
Without a humble but reasonable confidence in
your own powers you cannot be successful or happy.
—Norman Vincent Peale

My husband Brian is a skeptic. Not one of those nasty skeptics who argues and calls names, but rather one who doesn't give up on his search for answers. He would never deny his own experiences but will exhaust all options to find a scientific explanation for every experience he has. I am not sure how in the world he fell for me, because I have been "weird" since well before he met me. Somewhere along the line I decided that it must be my good looks, charm, and ability to make life interesting just by the pure nature of my being.

I have no memory of how I initially told Brian about my gifts. Neither of us remembers an awkward conversation while we were dating. Chances are, we were out having a few drinks and I blurted. Confession time, I am an intentional blurter—tactful most of the time, but a blurter nonetheless. It is a self-preservation tactic. I have conditioned myself to believe that if I blurt things out, people will be so shocked or startled that they'll have little to say in response. That is, unless they are a blurter too—then the conversation takes a sharp left and all chaos breaks out.

I may not remember our initial "I am a medium" conversation, but I do know the looks that Brian gives me when he thinks I am going too far outside the science box. He is not one to talk much about his feelings, but he can't hide them either. He has what he calls involuntary facial expressions: he reacts with a look even before he cognitively recognizes what I said. One of my least favorite of these looks is what I think of as the "fight starter." It's a questioning look that borders on judgment. His brow furrows a bit, and then one eyebrow rises about a half a millimeter, his mouth pulls to one side, his pupils dilate, and his eyes roll ever so slightly. It is the look I would expect if I'd said something completely ignorant. He has admitted to questioning the validity of my words sometimes as he searches for proof, but he denies that he is judging me. He says that he isn't thinking I am dumb or crazy, but there is a pattern. He seems to make the face only when I say something he doesn't agree with or for which he has no mainstream scientific proof.

My immediate response to the fight starter is an equally judging face followed by a growl that sounds vaguely like *"Don't judge me, I am not stupid! I am not crazy!"* I'm sure it sounds like I am possessed.

These exchanges are the culmination of one harsh reality that couples with differing spiritual beliefs can face. Many relationships like ours fail because people can't get past their differences. Brian and I have talked about how we both worry that one day it will drive a wedge between us. Personally, I feel like there is no winner, and never will be, in the science-vs.-spirituality debate. They are different belief systems and, as far as I am concerned, both right. I believe that mainstream science just hasn't caught up with or found ways to measure the power of the mind and spiritual gifts.

A few scientists out there are studying the science behind intuitive gifts, but it is not widely accepted in the scientific community. I hope that we will see it come together in my lifetime, but I doubt it will happen that quickly. Even so, I watch for the one scientific study that is going to show Brian, and everyone else, that my gifts are real.

I used to pray that, just once, Brian would get to experience what I do so he would believe me fully. That prayer was answered, though it didn't end as I had expected.

One night, we slogged off to bed after an exhausting day and were knocked unconscious by the sandman as our heads hit our pillows. Our bed faced a small window barely big enough for a person to climb through, and it was covered by blackout curtains made from old, black pillowcases. As if God were playing a cruel joke on me, I was born with eyelids that remain open slightly when I relax. Even when I try, I can't shut out the images in my room at night, and any amount of light in the room seems like an interrogation lamp shining directly into my eyes. The only solution for me is to create the complete darkness that I had previously learned to hate.

Like most people, Brian and I each have a favorite side of the bed, and I stick very closely to mine. I am a very still sleeper: I can almost always be found in the exact same position and spot that I was in when I fell asleep. Not so with Brian: he is all over the place at night, and if it were his choice, he would claim the whole bed as his own.

That night was extremely restless for me. I tossed and turned, waking up several times with the feeling that something was watching me. I turned to look at Brian, just in case he was staring at me, but he was sound asleep with his mouth wide open, drooling on the pillow: a true sign that he was completely out. I lay there for a while, feeling stiff and uncomfortable. The hairs on my arms and the back of my neck stood at attention, my body was itching, and my eyes searched the dark, trying to see which one of my friends was staring at me. I saw no one and nothing but darkness.

It was normal for me to feel like someone was watching me while I slept, but somehow this was different. The air in my room was heavy: the basement smell was more pungent than usual. Moist, warm air—like breath—brushed across my cheeks and filled my nose. I tucked my feet tightly under the covers, made sure no body parts were exposed, and with an abnormal amount of hesitation, went back to sleep.

A few hours later, I awoke suddenly with a very disconcerting feeling. I immediately looked at Brian. He was lying on his back. He never lies on his back. His eyes were focused intently above our bed. My head jolted in that direction as well, worried that there was a spider on the ceiling above me. Silly me. The heaviness in the room was much more intense now, my chest muscles had tightened, my heart was about to burst from my body, I was sweating, and every hair was now fully erect. I asked myself over and over again, *Is this a dream, or is this real?* I was hoping that it was a dream, a really, really bad dream.

A disturbingly large figure hovered over the end of our bed. It was bigger and far more terrifying than anything I had ever seen or felt in my own home. The figure lurched forward and engulfed the space above me. The air between us thickened until I felt like I was trying to breathe marshmallows. I turned back toward Brian, wanting him to help me and, more than that, wanting to make sure he was seeing this. Was this the moment where something from the other side would finally kill me? Not in the shower, like I'd always thought, but in my bed? I needed him to be my proof. I needed him to see the thing that killed me with his very own eyes.

I saw a brief look of panic cross his face, but just as quickly as it came, the look diminished. He shrugged his shoulders and let out a dismissive "Huh." *Am I dreaming?* I wondered again. *This can't be real, or he would be far more scared!* Brian, the man who screams and pushes me out of the way to escape haunted houses, rolled onto his side and went back to sleep while a monster lingered over our bed. I was left on my own, in my medium world. Again.

This creature's dark eyes stared at me as its hinged jaw opened to show off stubby teeth just two inches above me. It looked something like an enormous Chinese dragon, with red and blue scales covering a long body and large head. I remember vividly the mixed scents of sweat, hot morning breath, and salty tears as I froze there in my bed. Stunned, I murmured, "Go away!" over and over, louder and louder, "Go away! *Go away! GO AWAY!*" But it remained there until I grew so weak and tired that I drifted back to sleep. I remember the moment I just couldn't keep my eyes open any longer: everything seemed hazy, my vision began to lighten, a sense of peace came over me, and a bright white light glowed around everything in the room. I slept well after that, and I know now that the white light was the same protector who had been there in that horrible basement of my childhood.

This whole ordeal seemed endless but was only about three minutes in length. When I woke up in the morning, I turned to Brian and gently shook him awake.

"Honey, I had a horrible dream last night about a demon," I said. I knew it wasn't a dream, but I wanted to talk to him about it without getting the look.

I got a *very* different look. His eyes widened as I started to describe the demon. He interrupted to finish my sentence: "kind of like a Chinese dragon, with red and blue . . . ." He finished describing the exact creature that had hovered over our bed the night before. With a skeptical yet fearful twinge in his voice, he asked, "We weren't dreaming, were we?"

My response was simply, "No honey, we weren't. Welcome to my world."

I felt triumphant, but a twinge of worry came over me as I remembered Meg's reaction to "my world." The conversation that happened next sent me into a wind tunnel of confusion. Brian was already trying to find an explanation for what had happened. My heart dropped as he said, "Maybe we just had the same dream." I shook my head in disbelief. I think I was trying to shake that thought out of my head. Frustration started to set in. How could he think that was a realistic explanation? How did he not see what happened and realize it was real? *Uhhhh, really? No!* I thought, *Are you kidding right now? You saw that!* He eventually, hesitantly, resigned himself to the fact that we had indeed experienced this together. I resigned myself to the fact that we had been only momentarily on the same page.

I struggled for a while after that. I didn't understand why Brian wasn't scared of the demon or why he didn't recognize how terrified I was and help me. I obsessed over it for weeks, playing it over and over again in my head. Each time, Brian shrugged his shoulders and let out the same dismissive, "Huh." Eventually, more insight about our differing reactions came to me.

At the time this happened, I was struggling with a lot of new doubts about my life. I was struggling to allow other people to help me when I needed help. I flat-out refused most assistance. Like a defiant child, I wanted to do everything myself. I struggled with giving up control, something I had none of when the demon was lurking over my bed. I think the balance between control and flexibility is my lifelong lesson to learn. The demon, and Brian's response to it, was a message to me about my inability to control every situation and handle everything on my own. It was meant to show me that the things in life that scare me don't scare Brian, and vice versa.

About a month after the demon incident, I met with a pastor in our community to talk about her family business. We sat in her home, talking as I perched in a side chair and she rocked in a rocking chair. I wasn't attending church at the time because up to that point my experiences with churches—especially their leaders—had left me feeling dejected, judged, and uncertain about what to believe about the God other people accepted. With Jesus walking beside me, of course I believed there was a God, but I struggled with what that actually meant in the context of church and religion. *Is Jesus God or is he the son of God?* I wondered. *Why would God create me with these amazing gifts only to surround me with people who would tell me they were a sin?* Our business conversation turned personal and, in typical fashion, I blurted. I told her about the demon over our bed and what I thought it meant. I was floored by her response, although, looking back on it, I shouldn't have been. It modeled the pattern I had experienced with every pastor, minister, or church leader I had spoken with before: a deep pattern of judgment and superiority.

She looked me in the eye and told me that the devil was fooling me. She told me that God does not bring forth messages through fear tactics. I sat there thinking, *Other than most of the Old Testament, I guess.* She told me that I needed to pray for healing and go to church and repent for my sins against God. She reiterated that the devil was too close to me, working through my "gifts," and then she offered to do some sort of blessing over me. I can only imagine that it was going to be closer to an exorcism. Her insistence pushed me further away, and I declined as I got up to leave. The putrid smell of judgment filled that room. She looked at me as if she were staring down the devil in the flesh. Until that day, I had not doubted where my gifts came from. The idea that I was a sinner was another story. It tore me apart, piece by piece and memory by memory. I started to think about the fearful moments in my past, and more fear crept in. I worried that it really was the devil standing next to me rather than God. I considered this woman a friend; I wanted to trust her, but something inside me told me that what she was saying was wrong.

Still, I pushed Jesus away, afraid that I couldn't trust anyone. I shut down and started blocking the messages from spirit completely. I was unsure of myself and my gifts and confused about where the messages were coming from, but in that blocked state, I couldn't communicate with the few spirits who could actually help me. I had never experienced a full block of my gifts before this, and my mood turned pensive at the thought of losing them forever.

This state only lasted a few months. As I sorted through the fearful moments in my life, I was awakened to the fact that I needed to find a balance between my gifts and my belief of who God is. I learned that many others who share my gifts use them in ways that are not of the light, not for the higher good of anyone but themselves. I learned that everyone has a choice to be of the light or of the darkness, and that being of the light doesn't mean that you won't ever let the darkness in. We all make poor choices and step into our own shadows at times.

As I walked with my truth that year, I saw that the human world is meant to teach us about balance. Within each of us there is light and dark, yin and yang, masculine and feminine, our gifts and the shadows of our gifts. Our shadows only become problematic when we aren't embracing balance in our lives. The darkness cannot take over when we maintain a healthy balance. If we do things from a place of love and a place free of ego, we remain in the light.

When this pastor drew in to question my intentions, my character, and my messages, I felt called to be more present with what my path entailed. I felt called to speak it into the world around me. I wanted to embrace what I knew to be true of myself, fully. The day that I sat down and spoke my choice was the day I realized that she was wrong and I was always of the light. Even if the devil had been in my room that night or at moments before that, God was definitely the one who delivered my messages and surrounded me with the light of protection.

That pastor solidified my belief in my own spiritual gifts and the power of energetic healing. For me, her lecture solidified everything that she was trying to disprove. Her adamant position that my gifts were a sinful reminder of the devil's work in human lives set the tone for me to question the gifts of the pastors in the churches, the prayers that they speak, and the blessings that they provide. Why are their messages seen as a gift from God but mine a sinful message from the devil? My gifts are akin to theirs, slightly different but complimentary. As ironic as it is, I feel that this realization was the intended divine outcome of blurting my truth to her.

Many years later, my friend Krista invited me to attend a church service with her. She had just started attending and was finding peace for herself, so I begrudgingly went with her. It was more to support her than to support my own growth, but shortly thereafter, I began attending to gain a deeper understanding of my own faith. Within my first few weeks there, the pastor told the story of Job. He was a faithful man who followed the word of God with precision. As the story goes, Satan was allowed to take everything that Job had in an attempt to show God that Job would turn his back on him. God allowed Satan's attempts to prove a point. As the story continued, I thought about the demon over my bed. I thought about the words of that other pastor, years earlier. In that moment I started to believe that maybe I'd had my Job moment there in her home. Do you choose faith and the light, or do you walk away into the darkness? I have no doubt that I have always been of the light, so in that moment and every moment since, my faith and the light have won.

17

CHILDREN OF THE CORN AISLE

You've gotta wonder what kind of vibe you're putting out there if you're having really creepy people come talk to you.
—Jorja Fox

As we walk forward with our own lessons and realizations, we often have experiences that remind us that others are struggling as well. Sometimes those reminders come in an odd form or as mystical messages that we don't quite understand in the moment.

Throughout my teens and twenties, my mom and I often did the grocery shopping together. We would flit around the store, gathering what we needed and skipping the aisles we didn't need to go down to save time. It was not uncommon for us to have interesting interactions with strangers, most of which ended in my mom saying, "Did you know that person?" We both have an energy about us that draws information out of people, from life stories to obscure illnesses, the fact that they are getting a divorce tomorrow, the date of their next vacation, and so on.

For some reason, people immediately trust us. It is a fun gift to have. Some of my friends used to place bets on how much information people would give me in the first five minutes of a conversation. I never cashed in, but I am sure some of my friends made a pretty penny. So Mom and I knew that we would get a few overshare moments per grocery run, and I would end up hugging at least one perfect stranger. When people came up to us, we seldom batted an eye until that one day in the corn aisle.

It was an all-around bizarre sensation. We turned into an aisle halfway through the store, with sodium-laden canned vegetables on one side and boxes of cardboard-flavored meal mixes on the other side. Two children, a girl and boy, no more than six and eight years old, stood in the middle of the aisle. No adults in sight. No adults within three aisles, in fact. I can only assume, from the similarities I remember, that they were brother and sister. Their clothing, which seemed reminiscent of a different time, was all black and coated with a thick layer of dirt. The children stared straight at us as if we were a train plowing toward them on the train tracks. Normally, we would have thought nothing of kids in the grocery store: a smile and a little wave would have been exchanged, probably a cheery hello. This time though, we both felt the same thing: *something. wasn't. right.* The hair on my arms rose, and I felt that all-too-familiar fear sneaking in.

The way these children looked at us did not feel normal. Their eyes seemed silvery and hollow. As we approached, they opened their mouths and spoke in the most terrifying, *Children of the Corn* voices.

"Can you help us?"

The sister's eerie whisper came out with a one-second delay from her brother's, like we were in a canyon listening as they yelled over the edge. The tone was higher pitched and forced out air more than it should have. Images of the spirit children who often stood over my bed while I attempted to fall asleep flew into my brain like a swarm of angry bees.

My mom and I looked at each other, and fight-or-flight kicked in. We started walking faster. Neither of us knew why we were walking away from these children. For goodness' sake, they had asked us for help. We both love kids, and this was completely abnormal behavior for us, obviously brought on by fear of the unknown. Guilt and shame flooded my head as we turned the corner out of the aisle. My brain sought reasons that two kids would be dressed that way, why they were asking for help, and why they did it in such a creepy tone of voice. I started to question the reality of the space and time that we live in. Bad things happen to people, children included. Were they being kidnapped? Were they having a hard time reaching the cans of corn? Were they lost in the store? Or were they already dead? (I assume my mom had considered similar questions, but my thoughts always tended toward the obvious, to me, question of mortality.)

We stopped in the next aisle and asked each other, "What just happened?" Almost immediately, we both turned back to help those kids. The kids were completely gone! There was no trace of them. The trip around the corner had taken us five seconds, for four of which I had watched the kids to make sure they didn't chase us. We searched up and down the aisles, but they had vanished from the store.

This terrified us even more. The fact that I see and talk to spirits often (which my mom knew) made us question whether these were living children or spirits that were asking for help. To this day, we do not know what happened to the children of the corn aisle. We don't know who they were, if they were dead or alive, or if we could have helped them, had we kept our fear in check.

I am ashamed to admit that we bolted, but in that moment there seemed to be no other choice. Unfortunately, such situations happen when we don't have a way to learn about our gifts. This is a reality for many people who have the gift of mediumship. Until we are fully aware of our gifts, we often doubt what we see. It sounds outlandish to a lot of people to run away from helping children, but it is my bizarre truth, and it is shared by more people than are willing to admit it publicly.

The uncertainty of differentiating between living people and spirits started to feel normal after a while. It was in that state of dubious normalcy that I often forgot that I had no clue what I was actually doing.

As the years passed, there were moments when I thought I had it figured out. After all, I had been talking to spirits since I was a kid; I had to be an expert by now, right? Wrong! One thing I didn't realize until I was in my twenties was that you have to learn to protect yourself. It is just like walking across a busy road: if you don't take precautions, there is always a chance that you could get hit. I learned the hard way that not all spirits are harmless.

Eighteen years after the experience in the house on Thomas Avenue, I had yet another basement experience. Sarah had moved into an older home in St. Paul with her two children. She mentioned to me that she didn't feel comfortable in one area of her basement. As she gave me the tour of the house, we stopped to look at that one room.

I had already felt an energy that made me uneasy as we walked down the stairs. As she opened the door in the back corner of the basement, a wave of anxiety and fear swept over me. I almost expected to see the toilet seats, tall table, and chains from Denise's basement all over again. My mind clouded with horrific pictures of chained-up animals and women being assaulted. I saw dirty old mattresses lined up on the floor and chains strung from the pipes in the ceiling. I snapped out of the image to see an extremely angry man walking toward me. Like so many times before, I froze. Sarah was standing behind me in the doorway, and I hoped she couldn't see him.

He yelled at me, "This is my place! Get out!" I turned to Sarah and said, "I don't like it in here. Let's go." I surprised myself with the calmness in my voice, but Sarah saw through it when I high-tailed it up the stairs.

"What's wrong?" she asked. She seemed puzzled.

I blurted out, "I wouldn't go in that room."

The look of shock on her face told me there was more to the story. I explained portions of what I had seen. Then she told me that another friend had seen similar images of chains and animals in his mind when they toured the basement. That was confirmation enough for me.

I thought, *Nope. Not going anywhere near that room again!* I wanted Sarah and her family to be relaxed in their house, though, so I passed on a bit of advice I had received months earlier, at my very first psychic reading. This woman was the first person I'd spoken with in depth about my gifts. She was also the only psychic I had ever talked to, so I trusted any advice she gave me. "Boil rose petals and spray the water in your home to contain any spirit that you don't want roaming there," she had said. "You can also help stuck spirits cross over with love by using the spray as well."

Spraying rose water to help this angry man cross over seemed like a beautiful way to keep Sarah and her family safe. Helping a spirit cross over with love has to be a good thing, right? Unfortunately, Sarah listened.

About a week later, I had a very rude awakening. Still running solo in my quest for knowledge, I didn't know appropriate etiquette when dealing with a low-vibrational-energy entity, or negative spirit. The same psychic who shared the advice about rose water had also told me that spirits couldn't hurt people. I tried to believe her but continued to cope with the lingering fear of what might happen when I was alone in the shower or surrounded by spirits in my bedroom at night.

"They can't hurt you" she reassured me. "They just scare people from time to time."

That theory was wrong. I am convinced that those words could only have been spoken by a person who had never been confronted by a spirit with the will to hurt someone. Without proper energetic protection, I found out, spirits can indeed hurt people, especially if they feel taunted or provoked. If you don't know what you are doing, you should never mess with an energy that scares you. Fear can be a sign that you are not fully protected.

I got up the next morning and took my shower as usual: checking my blind spots, worried about who was going to sneak up on me. This time, someone was waiting for me. When I opened the door to the bathroom, the man from Sarah's basement was standing on the other side. My body betrayed me once again. I couldn't run, I couldn't close the door, I couldn't do anything. I froze as I looked into his angry face.

"That is my space! Leave me alone!" His face was red, his eyes were bloodshot, and his breath was sour like curdled milk. The look in his eyes was not that of someone willing to talk it through, but I "knew" he couldn't hurt me because he was "only" a ghost . . . after all, the psychic had told me so. I had myself convinced until he grabbed my arm. I started to panic.

"We didn't know it was your room, we just wanted—"

He cut me off. "You stay away from my room and leave me alone, and I will stay away from you!" He let go of my arm and was gone.

My panic grew stronger as I realized that I had sent Sarah down to the basement with rose water to help him "cross over with love." I knew this was all my fault. A feeling of dread and confusion came over me. I was supposed to know what I was doing! The only thing that gave me any comfort was the clarity that his words were directed at me, not at Sarah. It was as if he recognized that she couldn't see him and I could.

As I drove to work, I looked down at my arm. It still hurt, and I noticed that I was starting to bruise. I had learned a very valuable lesson the hard way: I had *no clue* what the heck I was doing, and I was right back at square one with no one that I trusted to ask. I felt like I was putting myself and others in danger because I was naïve. To top it off, I now had another thing to fear. This new discovery turned my already strict shower routine into a draconian law.

That night, my phone rang, and as I saw Sarah's name on my caller ID, my heart sank. She had boiled the rose petals the day before, put the water in a spray bottle, and started to spray in the basement. As she approached the door to the room, the sprayer on the bottle stopped working. She pulled the trigger over and over again. Nothing. As she walked farther away from the door, the spray bottle started to work again. She tested it out several times before running upstairs and deciding that she was just going to avoid that room whenever possible.

I didn't want her to be scared—I never wanted anyone to be scared—so I avoided telling her about my experience. I just agreed that she should not mess with that room anymore. From that point on, each time I entered her house I felt the rising energy of that man. It was a haunting warning to me: "Stay away from my room and leave me alone." I never went into that basement again, and thank goodness, Sarah moved.

After that experience, I really started to delve into the reason for all my fears. I had no idea where to turn, and I wasn't about to start asking random psychics after the last bit of advice I'd received!

When I turned thirty-one, I started to feel adventurous and contacted a healer that a client had recommended. It turned out to be one of the best choices of my entire life. The day of my session, I found myself lying on a massage table in her home, listening to her speak about the fractured pieces of past lives that were popping into her view. All of them depicted me bathing: in one I was in a waterfall, another in a cement shower house, and another in the shower of a very quaint farmhouse.

She had started by asking questions that, intellectually, made no sense to me. Yet, I could feel in my soul that they were connecting with something deep inside. She asked, "Do waterfalls mean anything to you?" I pulled a face and told her no, but inside I was struggling to keep the word *yes* from coming out of my mouth. I couldn't explain the feeling I was having. My heart was racing.

I was already pushing away from her questions when she brought up showers. "Do showers have significance in your life?" I cringed. I could feel myself stop breathing. My whole body became a deep, snake-filled pit of anxiety. I shuddered at the thought of standing in the shower, trying to avoid being murdered. I blurted out, "I hate showers." She seemed startled by my adamant loathing of cleansing myself.

I half laughed as I tried to explain that I didn't hate bathing but I did hate how I felt in the shower. She dug down toward the roots of my fear, and images of my past lives started to show themselves to her, and me. Over and over, I was attacked, strangled, grabbed, raped, or murdered at the hand of someone who suddenly appeared behind me as I bathed. The emotions that I was emitting in the visions were the exact emotions that I felt each morning as I stood in the shower. It explained so much, but I felt like there was no resolution in sight. If anything, I now had even more reason to fear taking showers.

Worry that my fear was about to get much worse gripped my body. My irrational fear had just gotten a little too real for me to handle. She laid her hands on my body, and an intense fight-or-flight sensation started to creep in. I wanted to run away, but instead emotions started to scroll through my body. Anger and then fear. Sadness, then discouragement. I knew that I couldn't get off the table and run, but I also knew I had no reason to fight her.

I started to cry, deep sobs that shook my soul. As my anger rose, she started singing a song by Alicia Keys, "Girl on Fire." Alicia Keys's music was not the expected cure for my emotions, but the timing was impeccable and the song seemed to take away some of the pain. My emotions turned to heat, and my usually cold body began to boil and sweat. Fear flashed in but quickly burned up in the fire that my body had become. Sadness flooded in, but it flowed in from the top, moved downstream, and was gone. The heat left with it, and discouragement took its place. The healer heard my body speak, and so did she. She spoke words into my being that assured me I would be okay. I started to feel as if, maybe, just maybe, it might be true.

After our session, the healer took time to teach me how to energetically protect myself in the shower. Together, we developed a new routine. The water would become a source of armor rather than fear. I would imagine that, as it rained over me, each droplet speckled my body with a beautiful white light. It thickened the armor and shielded me from the negative energies, from my memories, and from the pain. I felt ridiculous doing this. I thought back to the kids on the playground twirling their fingers around their ears, uttering the word *crazy*. I heard colleagues and friends repeating, "You are so weird." As I repeated their words to myself, I began judging myself as they had judged me. I felt crazy in this moment. I felt weird in this moment.

This is dumb, I thought. *This won't do a darn thing!* But I did it anyway because I wanted to get better. I wanted to heal, and even if I felt weird doing it, it made sense to me. I trusted this healer. The next morning I started using this new shower ritual. For the first time in thirty-one years, I didn't cry in the shower. I didn't curl up in a ball in the corner. I felt like I was finally getting better.

Over the next weeks, I jumped in the shower each day with my new routine, still expecting the fear to come back. Each day, the fear that had bordered on immobilizing dissipated more and more. Since then, I have only had three fearful shower incidents. Cue Dinah Washington's song "What a Difference a Day Makes." The showers that I once dreaded are now an average task, though I still use my old shower rituals out of habit. Armor up, white light washing over me, and then wash the hair on the back of my head, the left side of my head, and eventually the right side of my head. I recently started adding in a quick tip of my head backward to wash my whole head at once. As small as it sounds, it is a sign that I am finally over my fear of the shower.

I wish every emotion and every past life were an easy ritual away from being washed free from my soul, but I have learned that some things take deeper cleansing, a release, and a very close look at what I am actually hanging on to. Some things require that I change my perspective, if even just for a moment, in order to free myself from what has been keeping me stagnant. It is at those moments that I have to remember my life is not the reality of most and allow myself to step into a different reality in order to heal.

MESSAGES OF CLARITY

In this chapter you saw how important protection can be and how new routines or rituals can help calm the energy of the soul and create a protective barrier. Use the exercise below to create your own protection ritual.

Creative Imagery: Create your own image similar to the white light in my shower ritual to create a protective energy field around you.

1. Pick a situation in which you feel you need protection.

2. What tools or items are around you during this situation? (For me, it was water.) If you are outside, it could be clouds, air, trees, and so forth. If you are inside, it could be blankets, clothing, animals, or other things that are consistently present.

3. Which of these tools or items could easily surround you?

4. Imagine this item being filled with love and healing and engulfing you in its protective shield.

5. Envision yourself as completely surrounded with its loving and healing energy. Nothing can penetrate it without your permission, and nothing will be allowed through unless the vibration is that of joy or higher.

Each time you find yourself in the troubling situation, or any other situation of concern, use this image to protect your own energy.

18

WHEN LIFE IMITATES REALITY

As we live on this borrowed earth, using our borrowed time and the emotions of the ethers, we must set a precedent to live our lives to the fullest so that we do not waste our energetic resources.
—My Spirit Guides

Life has moments when reality falls just short of an abstract painting. Shapes and colors seem off, and yet they emotionally mirror the existence that we have come to accept. We examine this life, turning it around and squinting to make sure we are seeing the right things, all while maintaining a deep *knowing* that our experience is reality no matter how much we question it or how abnormal it seems. The paranormal world is like our human reality in that way. It seems to morph in and out of normalcy. When I think I am finally used to my world, a new gift pops up, a memory from a past life resurfaces, or I receive a message that changes everything.

It is in those "Oh my gosh, this really is my life!" moments that change and healing happen. Reality collides with my life head-on and creates an earth-shattering explosion on par with a hydrogen bomb. A surreal feeling seizes my body, and I have no choice but to pause to truly think about my existence. Those moments are not only explosive but also emotional and raw. They tear my insides apart with joy or fear or anxiety or . . . you name the emotion.

My most recent reality check came in the form of an unexpected past-life flashback in the middle of my workday. It was an extremely jarring flash, so emotionally charged that I could not focus for weeks. I would start a project and the images would pop into my head. A single word during a phone call would bring me back to those moments. They tormented me in the most powerful and intoxicating way. Blushworthy visions showed Symon, my husband from a lifetime lived in the 1800s, as we lived our life together. The visions beckoned me to relive moments of love, laughter, our child being born, playfulness, and pain, as well as his excruciating and unnecessary death. It played like a movie, over and over again. I was getting nothing done, and I didn't know how to stop the visions.

In these moments it was made clear to me that as humans, our souls always remember, even when our current bodies don't. My soul creates the passion in my life and the expression in my lifeless human body. It swells with emotion: fear, love, lust, excitement. It contains the memory of pleasures so vividly that it puts the ecstasy of human lovemaking to shame and mourns the sorrow of life more deeply than the depths of hell.

This past life was the epitome of those emotions for me. It was a life riddled with extreme love, over-the-top passion, and a sorrow that made my heart ache as if it had been torn out, dissected, and replaced after four days. I hurt because I longed to be loved like that again. I hurt because I was struggling to stay present in my own marriage while these visions were happening. I hurt because I was not currently receiving the love that I wanted in my life.

In that lifetime, I had been filled with unconditional love for others and shared my joy with not one person less than everyone. I was a ray of light for the town and a ray of light for Symon, although my family in that life frowned upon my marriage to him due to class.

As I remembered the moments of that life, I clung to the emotions and struggled with them. It was challenging not only because of the heartache I'd felt in the past but also because I felt an extreme sense of loyalty to Brian in this lifetime. I felt as if I were cheating on him emotionally as I relived moments of passion from two hundred years prior. Clarity formed, showing me that many of the circumstances in my marriage to Brian were directly related to the way that I had felt in my past lifetime. I was comparing Brian to a husband who had been dead for almost two centuries, and I needed to let go of that in order to make my current marriage better.

As a human, I have lived my life day to day, moving forward as if this one lifetime is all I have been given. I see people around me worry about aging and death, ignoring the soul's reminders to remember the loves that we have carried with us through eternity, reminders of the hundreds or even thousands of years of love and life that have been forgotten as we pass from one life to the next. All of them are waiting to be remembered. When those worlds collided for me, I was faced with a decision: let go and grow or hold on and risk stagnation.

I won't lie. I held on for far too many months, even after my guides firmly told me that my soul had to let go of my lifetime with Symon so I could move forward in the present one. I refused. I refused to accept that if I would just let go of the love I had felt then, I could have it in this lifetime as well. I felt like my life had become a circus freak show as painted by Picasso. A few of my intuitive friends knew all the details and understood why I was struggling. They watched me cry as I relived the past, moments I'd never wanted to return to again and moments I could have stayed in forever. They listened to the weakness in my voice as I waded through heavy emotions, and they shared in my ups and downs.

In the midst of this struggle, my company was scheduled to run a booth at a local psychic and healing fair. I was having a hard time keeping my focus and staying present, but I knew it was where I needed to be. My spirit guides prompted me to see a healer at the event to relieve the burden of my thoughts and the guilt and pain they brought. As I approached a random healer's booth, I began an aggressive inner dialogue with my spirit guides:

"I am not doing this. I am not ready to let go of this. I just want to feel loved like this."

Their response was quick and sharp. "You don't really have a choice. One of you will be making this decision this weekend."

At that point I became overwhelmingly aware that my soul was likely not the only one involved. His soul was out there, probably doing the same thing. A lump rose in my throat, and I felt tears coming to the surface. I could feel his soul, and he was struggling as much as I was. The only difference was that I knew why I was struggling, and it was very possible that his present self didn't.

I was afraid to let go because I was addicted to the warmth in my heart when I thought about Symon, the feeling of butterflies in my stomach when I thought about our past life together, the thought of his soft voice when he confessed his love to me in that lifetime, his laugh when we talked in the grass on the hill behind our house, and the feel of his hands, strong and slightly rough, as they brushed my hair away from my face to tuck it behind my ear before he kissed me. I knew that he would not return to my life as a partner, so, in theory, it should have been easy to let go of him. However, in my mind, letting go meant giving up all those memories and the feelings that came with them.

Slightly annoyed, the healer repeated to me, "Do you have questions?" I had no idea how many times she had asked already. I had been staring at this woman, watching her mouth move as she talked to me but not listening to her. I was fighting with my guides and trying to bury my grief.

"Tell me about the healing that you do," I inquired. I was not planning to listen; I just wanted to keep her occupied while I sorted through my choices. Move forward and lose this love again, or stay stuck and keep this wonderful feeling of being loved alive in my heart. My head was spinning. I didn't want to choose.

The healer's voice broke through: "Choose an angel card. I will tell you what it means." I reached out with my right hand to grab a card. "No, no, no," she scolded. "You must use your left hand, it is the hand of receiving."

I blurted out, "*Really?* I like to use my right hand for drawing cards!"

"Use your left hand," she insisted in a similarly harsh tone. Lacking the energy to argue, I switched hands and pulled a card. "The Archangel Uriel . . . Grace." The woman continued to talk, and I heard bits and pieces, words that reaffirmed I was meant to receive a healing from her, not because she was "the chosen one" to heal me but because she was the conduit that was standing in front of me at the time.

"How much do you charge?" I interrupted, and I barely waited for her response before adding, "Okay, do you have time right now?"

Looking back on it, I was a complete bitch to that woman. My inner struggles lent me no charm in that moment: my emotions were running at an all-time high, and my normal friendly attitude had turned to one of sarcasm and judgment since stepping up to her booth. I feared that the feeling of being loved, which I had been carrying for hundreds of years in the back of my soul, was nearing its end.

I sat down in the chair, and the woman blathered on about the different angels that she worked with. She asked me which one I wanted to have work with me that day. I didn't know, and I truly didn't care. I told her that whoever was supposed to work with me would step forward. I could tell she wasn't a fan of my answer. She was probably looking for guidance about what I wanted her to work with me on. She began her healing with almost no input from me, and I immediately left the human plane of existence. My soul had astral projected itself to another dimension to connect with Symon's soul. I was not expecting an out-of-body experience in the middle of an expo!

Our souls embraced with a passion that nothing would dare get between. He spoke softly in my ear.

"You know that I love you." He paused to let that sink in and then continued, "I always have and always will . . . We have to let go." Not the greeting I was expecting—he should have stopped at the pause. I stepped back from him and started to sob. My human body, appalled by his words, convulsed and recoiled away from the healer's hands. Tears tumbled down my cheeks. I knew that he was right, but I didn't want to. So I threw a temper tantrum.

"I don't want to. I can't lose you again. I won't go through it again!" He reached out and enfolded my hands in his.

"I want you to be happy again. You aren't happy now, and my soul can't give what you need." His eyes—a gorgeous light brown with a hint of hazel around the edges—looked sad. I didn't want to remember him this way. The look in his eyes was the expression on my face when I have failed at something, when I don't know what else to do. He continued, "It isn't the same when we aren't together physically, and we can't be in this lifetime. I just want to see you happy. The only choice is to let go."

His voice, slow and methodical, was like a chamomile bath, soothing as it rolled over my skin. He ran his left hand over my cheek and pushed my hair behind my ear. I dropped my head to the side into his hand as he cupped my face. Softly I said, "I can't do it." I looked up at him, hoping that he would just tell me that we didn't have to. When he didn't, I cried even harder, on the verge of hysterics. In my body, I heard the healer breathing as she tried to release what was streaming out from my throat chakra, the spiritual center for communication and truth. Every ounce of pent-up emotion was seeking release in that moment. I looked him in the eyes. They were loving and understanding; he could melt my heart with a glance, and he knew that. He always knew that. I felt our love even more deeply in that moment.

"I don't want to lose you again. It is like you are dying all over again." A slew of memories of his murder flooded my already overworked brain. I saw the faces and the blood; I remembered how I clung to his lifeless body in that moment, hoping it wasn't real. My shame was showing through. I had blamed myself for his death then, and I knew I would blame myself for losing him again if I let go. I could see his heart shatter when I said it.

He looked down at his feet and then back up at me. He slid his hands down to my sides and gently pulled me in toward him. "Remember the necklace I created for you?" he asked. His words were quiet and full of purpose. "It is symbolic of my unconditional love and protection. Now and forever." He had said it then, and he was repeating it now. "Know that when you see me, my soul will never forget my love for you. The soul never forgets, even if the mind does."

I fought a fresh wave of tears to say, "You are the only one who can love me the way that I need to be lov—"

He kissed me, his lips warm, soft, and extremely sweet. "Do you remember how you taught me to love to you? Do you remember telling me how you wanted to be touched?" I thought about it. I envisioned it. Tears still streamed down my cheeks as I nodded. He reached up and tenderly wiped the tears away. Tears were now filling his eyes as well. His voice broke as he said, "Teach your husband how to love you like you taught me back then. He loves you just as much as I do. He just loves you differently." I stared at him, memorizing every feature on his face, making sure that I hadn't forgotten anything. I knew that he was going to tell me to let go again. I could see the pain in his eyes.

His mouth opened slightly, and the words fell out. "We have to let go now. Remember that I will always love you." Those few sentences ripped through us like the teeth of hungry predators. I felt my heart stop for just a moment, and I felt sick to my stomach. A powerful sense of loyalty came over me; the problem was that I didn't know who it was to, Brian or Symon.

The healer's breathing was getting heavier, more intense; she pulled energy from my sacral chakra—the area of the body related to intimacy, connection, the ability to let go, and emotions. It was painful. Extremely painful. I held him tighter so that I wouldn't have to let go, pressing my face into his chest. His arms wrapped around me, and then I looked up at him. His eyes were glassy and tears were rolling down his cheeks as well. My heart was breaking.

Then I was back in my physical body, tears cascading down my face, fists clenched like I was still holding on to him. I looked at my hands and opened them. Too little, too late. I never let go.

The healer looked at me as if she knew what had happened. Her eyes looked sad, but nothing she said made any sense in conjunction with what I had just experienced. She was trying to make sense of my emotions, but it just made things far messier for me. I was still feeling torn between two lives. The healer identified the correct areas of concern, but it was all bullshit as far as I was concerned. She talked about how my throat chakra was blocked because I wasn't able to express my true purpose in life and I wasn't living my purpose. I thought, *No way, lady! My throat chakra is blocked because I didn't want to tell the one person I loved almost two hundred years ago good-bye again!*

She just wouldn't stop talking to me. I was so angry at her. I just wanted to cry. I needed to cry. I wanted nothing more than to walk away, but she wouldn't stop talking. Finally, she said something right: "Your sacral chakra was really blocked up, honey. You were hanging on to something so tight, and you wouldn't let go. It was as if you were afraid that if you let go you would lose something forever. I really had to work on it to disconnect it."

I heard the last part of her sentence at half speed. My anger boiled. *It is your fault that I had to let go!* I thought, raging. *You ripped him away from me!* I knew that was a lie I was telling myself so that I would feel better. I knew I had to let go. I knew that he had asked me to let go. I was supposed to let go, and I didn't.

My rage was coming out sideways, directed at her even though it was really meant for me.

The healer asked for validation, and I knew I had to keep it together. I told her that I was working through a past life and was struggling with that. No more details, no less. She gave me a look of disgust and disbelief. It was like she thought past lives sounded too crazy to be reality. Funny thought as we were sitting there, talking to the angels. My irritation and anger were growing more and more rapidly. I paid her, politely hugged her, and walked away, angry at her, angry at myself, and grieving.

My friends were waiting at the other end of the building. I couldn't look up at anyone as I walked there. I felt like a one-person freak parade on my own little torturous walk of shame. Everyone was staring, and everything moved in slow motion. I was dizzy and exhausted. My energy must have been horrible, and my face was red and likely puffy. As my friend Magdalena glanced up at me, I knew she could feel the change. I wanted so badly to cry—ugly cry—curl up in a ball and bawl my eyes out. I felt like my heart had stopped beating and my life was paused on the worst day of my existence. It was like watching Symon get murdered again.

I texted Brian to let him know I planned to go out with my friends after the expo. I couldn't go home right then. I needed time to process, and if I did fall completely apart, my friends were healers, psychics, and intuitives: I would be okay. At that point, Brian had no idea I was dealing with a past life, and to be honest, I wasn't sure how he would receive it. How do you tell someone that you love that you are having visions about someone else that you loved centuries in the past? That would go over like a lead balloon with my science-minded husband.

I floundered for the next week and a half. After I had time to think more about it, I started to realize that my guides knew what the outcome would be: one of us was going to choose to let go that weekend. It wasn't me. It was never going to be me, but they wanted me to see that I had the choice. They know that I'm stubborn, but hey, they tried to help. I came back to my body that day with my hands clenched just as tight as I could make them.

One important choice was missing from my inner dialogue. It never occurred to me that one of my choices was to choose not to let go and have his soul choose for me. Nor did I ever think that he would choose to let go himself. I thought, *This is what abandonment feels like. This is what it feels like to think that someone doesn't love you anymore.* Not even with my first breakup in this lifetime had that feeling entered my body and taken over my heart so completely.

I know that Symon's soul saw that I would equate that interaction with abandonment. I had equated his death to it all those years ago, although I blamed myself for abandoning him when I couldn't stop his murder. After that healing, my heart still fluttered a little when I thought about the images I had seen. I still had the visions, and my guides finally confessed that neither of our souls really let go that day. I was just meant to learn from the abandonment that I felt so I would choose to move on. My guides didn't realize just how stubborn I can be. I hung on even after the feeling of abandonment set in.

Many of my past lives have cropped up over the years. I have had no problem letting go of the energy behind most. *Acknowledge it and let go,* I tell myself. *Easy peasy.* This lifetime was different. All the other lifetimes had negative or indifferent feelings attached to them. This one did not: it was filled with the most intense love that I have ever felt.

How was I supposed to let go of something that didn't exist in this lifetime? How was I supposed to let go when my soul was still connecting with another soul now housed in a body that was no longer in partnership with me? How was I to ask my soul to catch up to my current reality and let go of something that was so beautiful at the time it was created? The truth? I needed to finally allow myself to see the full truth of the past in conjunction with my current reality.

As I waded through the visions of that lifetime as well as other lifetimes I had shared with Symon's soul, I found that I had censored the moments that created pain in my heart. I took in the images and locked them away as tightly as I have my anger, terror, and pain in this lifetime. I had visions of multiple lifetimes in which our souls had created a life together, and I changed the proverbial channel. Good times and bad times remembered. Bad times filed away in their own little safe. Multiple lifetimes of pain and joy. Images of our love, images of extreme bliss, images of Symon drunk and angry, images of emotional abuse and violence. I pieced together many patterns that I have relived over and over again as I tried to fill a void that I had not even known was there.

Those patterns were created and then began to disintegrate as my soul recognized the source of its pain and finally allowed itself to start to heal. My current lifetime was the dealbreaker for me. It held space for the moment I was meant to realize that the fire in my heart was not love but a longing for it. It was a longing for Symon to absolve the pain that I felt by replacing it with an equal amount of love through joyful memories of the one lifetime we shared in which he did not hurt me. This lifetime saved a space for me to recognize that my pain was not meant to be absolved by him; rather, it was to be resolved within myself. My current reality could not allow our souls to continue the cycle. The patterns needed to change in order for both of our souls to heal. As simple and commonsense as it seems, I learned that love and pain do not balance each other out over time when more sorrow is created with each step. My past-life sorrows far outweighed the love that I received, and yet it was still extremely hard to let go.

The memory of the pain forced me to withdraw; it wore me down and forced me to embrace it like a drunken lover, beautiful in the moment but a hideous mistake in the light of day. I had to learn to embrace my pain from the past in order to allow love in the present. I feel as if pain were the universe's last attempt to help me choose to free myself of the burden of my soul memories. Without discomfort, I would have continued my refusal to move forward.

I knew that pain creates growth and motivation for movement. To catapult forward I needed some type of a push, in this case the creation of new painful experiences, rejection, and a fear so strong that it created a paralyzing shitstorm of emotions that couldn't be quashed, no matter how hard I tried. The pain filled my mind with doubts so deep that I was unsure if my life had any meaning left at all. My soul dropped to its knees, pleading for mercy and wishing for hope, while I felt as if there were none. Without pain I would stand motionless, stagnant in my joy. Life would breathe on at a comfortable pace with little change, and joy would become monotonous, more habit than pleasure. Without pain I would no longer feel the yin and yang of life. I would no longer have choice and no longer live with motivation to create something better for myself.

My soul longs to be loved and yearns to forget the images that are forever burned into my mind. I pray that one day I will forget Symon and the love of that lifetime. I hope that I can forget the pain that it has caused. However, I know the memory of those things is necessary to propel me forward, and I have accepted the burden of the memories as a reminder of where I have been and what I must continue to grow from. I have chosen to distance my mind from the soul of the man I loved two hundred years ago so that I might move on peacefully, without guilt for still loving him now.

I had been thirsty for peace of mind and clarity in my own soul, but in order to quench that thirst, I needed first to walk away from that deep well of all-encompassing love. I needed a new source from which to drink, and that source was my current reality, my current relationship with Brian. The fear of dehydration consumed me, and my muscles weakened and withered as my body prepared for a drought that might or might not be coming. I had to look deeper into my relationship with myself and with Brian. I finally accepted that my well had drawn sorrow masked as love for years. I observed that my image of what love is had been skewed for so long that I truly didn't know what love looked like.

A few weeks after the expo healing, I found myself drawn to attend an interfaith church service. A woman was poised in front of the congregation, singing a soulful song she had written. My mind had focused on the beauty of the singing and ignored the lyrics, but my ears tuned in suddenly as she sang, "Let go now." Tears bubbled to the surface and worked their way down my face as an image of Symon flashed through my mind. He was looking me in the eyes, lovingly, with a slight smile on his face. As I tried to direct my attention to the rest of the words in the song, my soul was transported to a large, empty room. It was a very clean and white, with nothing in it but Symon's soul. We were already holding hands, and my words were swift and sincere.

"It is time to let go now." He nodded, and, for now, it was done. I was back in my seat at church, my shirt soaked with tears and my eyes wringing out every last bit of moisture that they could find to expel.

As if that weren't enough for one day, I had signed up for a healing from a large group of healers at the church. I entered a room with seven healers and started to unravel what was left of my scattered emotions. One of the women explained that I had been hanging on to far too much pain and anger, but my body was finally ready to let go. *Finally,* I thought.

As I lay on the table in the healing room, I struggled to find something to let go of. I had just let go of Symon, freely and by my own choice this time. I felt like there was something more around it but didn't know what. Searching for anything that needed healing in my life, I tried to picture Brian and our relationship. I couldn't. I panicked. Why couldn't I visualize him? Then I had a flash of Symon, drinking, from yet another lifetime. He was not a happy drunk by any means, and my soul was angry at him, still. I felt the anger surface and told myself to let go. Again, I cried. The healer told me my emotions were like a smokestack that had started to let out all of the smoke. It was a constant stream that would continue its release for a while.

It was just the beginning of my healing process. It was also the beginning of a new type of love for both my husbands, past and present. It was a time for forgiveness and acceptance for one and passion and truth for the other. For months I continued to seek resolution to my longing to be loved by Symon's soul. I crowded my mind with blissful images of him. Experience has taught me that when I think my journey is over, it more often than not is just beginning. I thought that I had let go as the images had faded away for a month, but they soon returned, more intoxicating, more passionate, and more intense than ever. I started to remember even more details of that lifetime. The images and my feelings of that time seemed to explain situations that were currently playing out in my life. I found that I was surrounded by people who house the souls of family, acquaintances, and friends from that lifetime. I started to piece together their roles in each lifetime and how they affected me physically, mentally, emotionally, and spiritually.

Unexplained anger I felt toward specific people in this lifetime corresponded to events from that lifetime. I felt peace and deep trust around someone I had no reason to trust, and an unusual feeling surfaced when one person knew my favorite color and sense of humor the first time we met. Some of my anger dissipated as I saw that the reason for my anger had long passed. My ability to fully trust people started to open up as I saw who they really were. I began to let my guard down as I saw my friends from the past, my soul friends, showing me that they were still here and still cared about me.

The memories of Symon still linger in my mind, but the lessons they taught are becoming more clear. My soul obviously fought to hang onto them for a reason. I was afraid to lose the sense of love that came with the memories, and I was not done learning from them, either. The memory of Symon brings joy to my heart. The lessons from his memory allow me to see Brian for who he is and not against the unfair standard of my past.

I know that I am loved now, then, and forever, but that does not change the strength of the pain I felt in letting go. It was akin to a divorce of souls, and releasing that kind of pain takes time. These lessons have given me reason to look at my life and have brought me closer to Brian. They were the catalyst for me to make changes, to step out my comfort zone and fully live my life. It was the giant neon "Open" sign hung on my soul to let everyone know that I was finally willing to ask for help and show my vulnerability.

My soul's life has been an infinite loop of lessons as it traveled from one lifetime to the next in hopes that I could learn what I was meant to learn from each of them. I had to grasp the idea that I must not be ashamed to accept who I was in those lifetimes or who I am in this lifetime. I must accept those who have walked beside me and remember that they, too, have lessons to learn or to teach. My anger, fear, resentment, pain, joy, and other emotions are merely tools to give me insight about my soul's purpose on this earth. Nothing more. Nothing less. I, as a human being, am the temporary container for a soul that has a far bigger purpose than a single lifetime of emotions can possibly show me. For that reason, I must continue to learn and grow from each of my lifetimes, even if it means reliving the pain for a second time (or third or fourth).

My past-life experiences have been an amazing gift. I now see the repetitions my soul created in order to enable me to become my own teacher. They have also helped me to see the stagnation that can occur if I get stuck in the past and accept the outcomes that I no longer control. I allowed myself to remain stuck, and then I got lost in the maze I created to shelter myself from my own lessons.

When I finally found my way out, I found that everyone was sitting around asking, "Where have you been?"

19

WHERE HAVE YOU BEEN?

> *Every new beginning comes*
> *from some other beginning's end.*
>
> —Seneca

My business was always a good way to distract myself from the lessons that I was too stubborn to face. When I found new lessons rearing their heads, I often buried myself in work. When that was no longer enough to mask my issues, I started a hobby of looking after homes and animals when people I knew were out of town. I did this so often that for several years I lived more in other people's homes than in my own. It was rare that I felt uncomfortable because my gifts ensured I always had someone to talk to and my hobby ensured I always had an animal to pet. Just like at home, though, the spirits found it hilarious to startle me by appearing out of nowhere at the most inopportune times: when I was getting out of the shower, as I washed my face in the sink at night, or more often than not, when I was walking through a dark room.

It was late September, and the temperatures were fluctuating, as they do in Minnesota. Although it was a warm sixty-three degrees outside, the wind kicked up and made frostbite seem inevitable. I was watching a home that I had been in thousands of times since I was a kid. It was a beautiful, large place surrounded by woods that kept it fairly secluded but also dropped the temperature a few degrees. My job for the week: come in from work, play with an adorable dog, feed her, and then go to sleep. It was just horrible, let me tell you!

On day five of my seven-day stay, I pulled up, opened the garage, and walked up to the door to the house. I was calm, collected, and super excited to play with the dog, as usual. Everything seemed one hundred percent normal until my hand hit the doorknob and my stomach started to churn. I slowly opened the door. The house felt different. It felt like someone was there. It didn't feel bad or scary at first—just that there was another presence. I ran through the days of the week: *Yup, it is only Friday. They aren't supposed to be home until Sunday. Nope, I didn't get a phone call telling me they would be home early, and there are no messages saying someone was coming over.* As far as I could figure, no one should have been in the house.

I entered the mudroom off the garage, and the dog lazily greeted me at the door. As soon as I set down my purse, I heard a female voice coming from around the corner in the kitchen and then cooking noises: pots clanking, water running, and a knife chopping vegetables.

"Where have you been?" the voice asked, clear as glass. Her tone was sweet and motherly.

Is there a person in the house? I thought. *Who is this person? That doesn't sound like any of the family members!* Normally the spirit voices I hear are muffled and distant, like they are talking through a telephone with a bad connection. *She has to be a live person.* I panicked.

My heart was racing, and I started to sweat and shake. I was having a hard time breathing. Not since the demon over my bed had I felt this much fear. But the dog barely even looked up when she talked, and animals are normally a good indicator of good vs. bad energies.

About forty-five seconds after I heard the voice, I finally regained my composure and forced out, "H-h-hello? Is someone here?" There was no response. "Hello? I heard you talking just a little bit ago." Still no response. My fear was getting worse, but I had no choice but to peek. With one hand on the dog, I snuck around the corner and saw nothing: no dishes on the counter, no pots that could have clanked, and no woman. "Hello?" I yelled. She didn't answer. I grabbed my purse and flung the garage door open again. The dog and I were out of there! *Hell if I am staying here tonight or ever going back in that house again by myself!* I thought, and I called my mommy.

After I told my mom what had happened, I begged her to come over. I had to feed the dog, and I refused to go back in there by myself. Loving mom that she is, she graciously agreed to come over after work. Mommy to the rescue! It was just like when I was a child: I saw something scary and cried to my mom, and she did her best to rescue me without judgment. The dog and I spent the next hour and a half playing in the yard. The temperature was dropping and I was getting cold, but I was not going back in that house by myself.

Mom arrived and walked into the house with me. With downturned eyes she said she didn't feel anything strange. I could tell that she felt bad admitting it. I am sure she didn't want me to feel crazy. I didn't feel anything anymore either. The odd sensation was gone from the house. I fed the dog, but I still couldn't make myself stay there alone at night. For the remaining days, Brian was my chaperone and bodyguard, even though he would have been far more frightened than me if something had happened while we were there.

The next year, the family asked me to watch the house again, and I agreed. In that time I had blocked out my last experience in the house. That is, until the dogs (they had multiplied in that last year) started acting odd.

I was sitting at the dining room table. Over my typing, I heard loud, clomping footsteps in the hallway upstairs. One of the dogs charged upstairs. I can only imagine that he was trying to protect me from the intruder who dared to disturb our peaceful evening. This dog is very predictable and isn't afraid of anything. He loves everyone and would make friends with any stranger on the street. He was upstairs for a total of five seconds, and then he let out one short bark and galloped through the house like a stampede of miniature ponies. I got up from the table and ran over to the steps just in time to see him come tearing around the corner and down the steps to disappear under the dining room table. It worried me, and the other dog, that he was so panicked.

The dog set up camp under the table for hours. No amount of treats or love was going to get him to abandon his refuge. So I, like an expendable character in a scary movie, made the intelligent decision to check it out. I slowly walked up the stairs to look around. Once again, I saw nothing but felt something there. That something moved quickly behind me to the top of the stairs. Everything felt cold and mysterious. I ran back down the stairs, and as soon as I turned the corner into the dining room, I heard *thud, thud, thud, bounce, bounce, bounce, bounce*. It sounded like a ball hitting each step on the way down and continuing across the wooden floor.

I looked around the corner and saw nothing on the wood floor that could have made that noise. I snuck over to the bottom of the steps and searched on my hands and knees for anything that could have made the noise. I was convinced that I had just knocked something down as I ran down the steps, even if the timing was off. After what seemed like an hourlong scavenger hunt, I walked away with absolutely nothing to explain the noise. I headed back into the dining room, where the dog was still shaking like a chihuahua in the rain and staring at the stairs. Nothing was moving that dog, and I was starting to feel like crawling under the table with him. Whatever he saw, I really didn't want to see it either!

Later that night, I cautiously went upstairs to bed, dogs in tow. The dogs jumped up in bed with me. I hesitantly turned off all the lights and curled up in a fetal position under the covers. I was exhausted, so sleeping sounded like heaven, but I was only asleep for a few hours before I was startled awake by something shoving the dog into me, hard. It was not a motion that the dog should have been able to do on his own: he was lying on his side and was pushed at least a foot across the bed in order to hit me. Both of the dogs perked up and started to growl. The one that had hidden under the table looked at me with the same fear that he had in his eyes earlier. I pulled both of the dogs closer to me and wrapped my arms around them, and, uncertain, they started to relax again. Eventually they laid their heads down, one on each side of me, and fell back to sleep. I tried to convince myself that a vivid dream had catapulted the dog into me, but after lying still for a while, I started to analyze what it would take for the dog to move himself a whole foot in my direction at that angle. That, and the reaction of both dogs, made for a hard sell. As I was working that out in my head, I realized that I could feel something in the room with us.

My cell phone has a plethora of uses. Not only is it my panic button when I get scared and want Brian to come save me, it is also my camera and alarm clock. For that reason, I had my cell phone under the pillow next to me on the bed. I slowly reached for it, flipped to my camera, and started taking pictures of the darkness in the room. I immediately started to feel uneasy about it. A deep voice boomed, "No more," and I put my camera away. When told what to do by faceless, nameless spirits I don't generally do what I'm told without question, but this was a different scenario. This felt like ignoring the request would have consequences.

I could feel someone standing over me. The feeling itself wasn't unusual—I was used to that from childhood—but the darkness of the room was pale in comparison to the darkness of the shadow I saw backing away from the bed. Thank goodness it was heading toward the door and not closer to me. An uneasy feeling was forming rapidly. I started to itch. My mind wandered to the itchy gods from my childhood, and I felt the need to protect myself and the dogs. I envisioned myself surrounded in a giant bubble of white light. Then I asked the angels and God for protection, and a much larger gridwork of thick ropes made of light surrounded my bubble. This beautiful cage looked as if it had been woven from the power of angels and God himself. I felt protected, I felt peaceful, and I felt . . . sleepy.

The next morning when I got to work, I decided to take a gander at the pictures from my phone. I was shocked when I saw a multicolored form resembling an extremely chubby butterfly at the end of the bed, halfway up the wall toward the ceiling. I was convinced that I had caught something paranormal in my photo but was unsure of what it could be. It didn't look anything like the sinister shadow that lurked in the room, and I hadn't seen any light in the room that night.

I called my friend Magdalena for a second opinion. Her normal was my normal, so I could tell her the full story and expect an honest opinion. I had no experience with paranormal investigation, so when I asked her to look at the photo I wasn't expecting her suggestion that a small investigation might be in order. Thank goodness the owners of the house had given me permission to have her and another friend, Alex, out to the house. I hoped that if they came in, the spirits in the house would finally have an outlet to say what they needed to say, to someone who wasn't me.

After Magdalena and Alex looked at the photo of the chubby butterfly, they joined me at the house. We found a knickknack on a shelf at the same level as the chubby butterfly from the picture. As best we could determine, the colors may have been a reflection of moonlight through the window that night. However, we could not recreate it. There may have been more to it than that, but will never know for sure what it was.

We did a walkthrough of the house, and they pulled out some of their investigating equipment: K2 electromagnetic field meters, flashlights, audio recorders, and, of course, the old-school notepad and pencil. I was excited because it was the first investigation that I had ever been on, even if it wasn't exactly official. We settled in the living room, and my excitement grew when they gave me permission to help.

The process of investigating was far different than I expected. In my head, it was like the paranormal investigation shows on television: jam-packed with evidence, voices, noises, furniture moving by itself. . . . It isn't like that. Well, it isn't like that all the time. The shows take an enormous amount of footage and cut it down to an hour of only the "good" parts. When you are actually investigating, you ask a ton of questions and then wait. And wait. And wait some more. What the shows don't tell you is that the amount of energy a spirit expends to communicate is immense. For me, it would be like running a mile when I haven't eaten in a week. Also, there is a learning curve. Sometimes it takes the spirits quite a while to learn how to use the tools in the room as an energy source. It depends partly on how many lifetimes (and deaths) the soul has been through. When they figure out how to use the tools, it is amazing! As we sat there waiting for the responses, I remembered how much William had strained trying to move the straw, how exhausted he was afterward, and the look on his face when he finally did it. The process was all starting to make sense to me now.

Magdalena and Alex set up a few flashlights on a table in the living room in hopes that the spirits would figure out how to answer simple yes-or-no questions by turning the lights on or off. The spirits understood and jumped at the chance to communicate with us. I am sure there were far too many giddy squeals on the recording from me when the lights confirmed information that I was receiving directly from the spirits there.

While many people are hesitant to accept the flashlight method as proof of communication with spirits, after having been in the room and having witnessed the undeniable timing of the responses, I am a believer. As we sat in the living room and I watched the spirits play with the flashlight, I was overjoyed. They beamed when they saw that the three of us were responding to them. They felt like they finally had a larger voice. It was truly amazing.

We asked question after question for a few hours that night. About twenty minutes in, I started to hear names of the spirits waiting to talk to us and saw the line of people waiting to speak. All three of us felt the energy of the people who were there, those who wanted to speak and those who wanted us to leave. Suddenly, I started to feel as if I couldn't breathe. My chest got extremely heavy, and I gasped for air. I opened my mouth to explain to Magdalena and Alex what was happening, but tears were welling up in my eyes from the sadness and fear that I was feeling. Then an excruciating pain came over me.

Thomas, the spirit we were speaking to at the time, was using my body as a prop to show us how he died. I wasn't expecting him to do it, but this was a fairly normal experience for me. I thought it was just a normal part of the way I communicated with them. It may not have been the most pleasant way, but it worked.

Magdalena and Alex had far more experience in the professional realm of working with spirits than I did. I was, in my own head, just an amateur. As I explained to them what was happening, Magdalena shook her head and without hesitation asked the spirits to use the energy from the lights and the equipment rather than from me. I was shocked. I didn't know that anyone else knew this could happen! I thought, *They know about this! It happens to other people, it isn't just me!* That moment sparked a message that it was time for me to set healthy boundaries with the spirits who were communicating with me.

Thomas started to use different tools to show me his message. He gave me the image of a man in a blue-grey Civil War military uniform. It was extremely dirty and wet, as if he had been lying out in a field in the rain. There was blood covering his jacket, but I could not see where the blood was coming from. I could feel a sharp pain in my abdomen that radiated up into my chest. My breathing became more labored the more I vocalized the images that I was being shown. The pain was becoming much more intense. The muscles in my jaw tightened and my legs started to quiver, no doubt a symptom of this man's pain. I started to get weepy. As I explained what was happening, Magdalena blurted out two names that she was hearing: Sarah and Charlie.

Those were the names of my best friend and her daughter, who were then sitting in a hospice facility with Sarah's grandmother as they prepared for her passing. They had been on my mind, naturally, but of all the names that could have come through just then, why those two? The spirit realm and my human reality were blending together in such a way that I wasn't sure what the message was. I texted Sarah to see how her grandmother was doing. She wasn't doing well, but there had been no significant change in her condition. After that, the names didn't come up in our investigation again that night.

We continued with our questions for the gathered spirits. The flashlights were going absolutely crazy, and the responses matched the information I was hearing . . . and blurting out. The spirits answered most of the questions with little hesitation. I was so thankful to finally have some extra confirmation on the information that I received. For once, I didn't feel crazy!

With all the excitement of the evening, I had one question that I wanted answered. To ease my own mind, I wanted to know who the woman was in the kitchen the prior year and why she asked me where I had been. I was ecstatic when she responded to us, but the flashlight confirmed the heartbreaking words I had heard.

Her name was Margaret. She was the mother of a beautiful, active, ten-year-old girl named Elizabeth. As Margaret stood in the kitchen, making dinner for her family, Elizabeth was out in the yard playing. Margaret called to her to come in for dinner, and she never responded. She never came home. Each night, Margaret replayed this scenario in her head in hopes that, one day, Elizabeth would walk through that door and her mother would get to ask her, "Where have you been?" She longed to hold her daughter one more time. She wished that she could see her walk through that door with her clothes muddy and grass-stained from a long day of jumping in puddles. She just wanted her child to come home, and my silent response to her question was one that she had heard each night since that somber day.

Stories like Margaret's create sadness within me, and in those moments, I have a hard time wanting to use my gifts—not because I can see the pain that the spirits still carry, but because most of us, as humans, like to believe that once someone passes away, they are free from all pain, emotional and physical. It is a lie that we tell ourselves so that we feel slightly better when we lose a loved one. Sometimes it feels better to be naïve than to allow ourselves to see the truth. Sometimes spirits don't let go right away. Sometimes spirits need help from people like me and my friends to help them release their emotional ties to the physical world and move on.

Our human emotional state imprints itself on our soul, and as our soul uses our physical body as a vessel to house itself, it overlays the imprinted pain, grief, fear, or any other strong emotion we carry onto that physical body. Think about when you get nervous about giving a presentation. Your emotional state, the nervousness, creates a response in your body. Some people shake, others get nauseous, and some sweat. If you have a poor outcome from your presentation, that emotional response often carries over to the next presentation. Repeat it often enough, and the response becomes imprinted on your being—you will continue to respond with the same nervous response until you learn your lesson and take steps toward healing.

Most souls have work that needs to be done in order to heal

their emotional pain before they are ready to move on to the next lifetime—the next presentation. In some cases, the soul will carry a pattern of pain or discomfort through multiple lifetimes before it is fully healed, and some healings are easier than others.

Our soul assists in choosing the lessons we are scheduled to learn in each lifetime, but as we walk in a new body, most of us don't consciously carry this knowledge. Emotions at the human level are very raw and close to the surface. That energy is like a memory that you cannot forget, no matter how hard you try. There is no hiding from emotions. They are part of what creates our soul's personality as well as our fears, our passions, our quirks, and our faults.

By recognizing the responses of the physical body and the emotions we experience, we can start to release the energy of our emotional imprint and heal at a soul level. It works the same in spirits. If they can acknowledge their emotional pain and move on from it, they will no longer have to carry the lesson forward to each lifetime.

After Margaret told her story, she began her healing process. She started to release the emotional imprint that she was carrying with her and finally move on. My eyes were opened to how human we remain after we shed our physical bodies. Even after years of listening to the stories of the spirits around me and talking to William on a regular basis, I hadn't fully understood the extent of the emotions that could be carried over after death. It certainly made me start asking some hard questions: What will I carry with me? What lesson do I need to learn so my soul can be free? How can I start my healing process now?

MESSAGES OF CLARITY

Throughout my life, there have been many times when I should have asked for help. Fear and repetition of unpleasant situations are often signs that it is time to get assistance or healing from someone else. The longer I work with my gifts, the more I have come to realize that I can't handle everything alone, and I now know that I don't want to. Learning to protect myself and my energy and to ask the angels, my guides, and other intuitives to step in to help once in a while has allowed me to walk through my own life with more confidence and less fear. There are things in the spiritual realm that we are not meant to handle alone because they trigger something in us that needs to be healed or are energies that we shouldn't be working with without backup.

1. Take a moment to think about your life and the lessons that your soul is meant to learn this time around.

2. Where in your life do you struggle with fear?

3. Where in your life do you see patterns of repetition?

4. What lesson do you think your soul is choosing to learn from the fear and repetition?

5. Who will you ask to assist you with your healing?

20

LOST SOUL

You don't have to have anything in common with people you've known since you were five. With old friends, you've got your whole life in common.
—Lyle Lovett

Over my lifetime, I spent more time talking to William than to anyone else I know, living or dead. He was my constant companion until 2015. He knew everything about my life. He would wake me up when I accidentally slept in, play with my dog and keep her company if I was busy, and bother me like a naughty child if I wasn't giving him enough attention. At times he was like my little brother, and at other times I felt more like his mother than anything else.

He would disappear for weeks at a time, maybe a month, but he always came back. During those long times away from him I would start to fear that I had lost my gifts. In one of those periods of scarcity, I went to psychic medium to ask about him. She very matter-of-factly told me that in a past life, I was his mother. Her words resonated with me, but I couldn't find any evidence. Up to that point, he had never given me any indication of who he was or why he was always with me. Regardless, I accepted him as my long-lost son and just let that idea stew in the back of my mind for years.

In 2015, I had a conversation with William that ended with his real story—or at least part of it, anyway. He spoke very quietly as he told me about his soul journey so far. I had never heard him speak so softly before. He would whisper at night when he was trying to wake me up, but this was a muted and much gentler tone. I guess it wasn't the volume that was different; it was the emotion behind it.

"I've been waiting a long time to come back and see you," he said, almost overcome by emotion. His eyes widened as any excited kid's would. He continued, "I'm ready to come back now."

I didn't understand at the time that our souls come back when they are ready to learn more. William wanted to be born and had been given the opportunity to be born into a family close to me. When it came time to prepare his soul to come back, however, there was a medical concern. Due to complications with conception, the pregnancy was deemed risky. The mother's doctor made a recommendation that due to the high risk to her and the likeliness of birth defects, the fetus should be aborted. That is, William's new human body should be aborted.

I can only imagine how hard that conversation was and the time that it must have taken to decide. I can hardly surmise how William's soul felt as he listened to the decision-making process. It was painful on both sides. The couple eventually made the heartbreaking decision to take the doctor's recommendation, and the baby—baby William—was sent back to the spirit realm. William told me that at first he was devastated that he was unable to come back at that time. He thought that he would get to see me in this lifetime as a "real boy." However, that was not in the cards this time around. He then explained that he forgave the parents for their decision and now understood why they made that choice. He told me that there was a bigger picture to take into account. However, he didn't say what that bigger picture was.

I reluctantly shared William's story with the would-be parents. After that, William disappeared. My role all along may have been to help him forgive as well as to give the parents a little bit of peace about their choice. I accomplished both, but I miss him.

I often wonder where he ended up. Was he born back into this world, or did he just give up on seeing me again? No matter his reason, I miss him.

It wasn't until I started having the past-life flashbacks in early 2017 that I found out the rest of William's connection to me. The flashbacks were fraught with pain, turmoil, and sadness, but also an amazing amount of joy. I saw images of my past-life husband, Symon . . . and our family, and I realized that this was the only lifetime I had regressed back to in which I had ever seen myself with a child of my own. He was a beautiful, talented, and happy blond-haired boy who took after his daddy.

The flashes of Symon's violent death were followed by months of images that showed me the turmoil of the time and, as an aside to the rest of the story, the soul of this young boy. It took me weeks of seeing them to acknowledge that this boy was William. He was my child in *that* lifetime. I *was* his mom. And I sensed that he was the only child I had ever birthed, in any lifetime.

It all clicked in that moment: The medium telling me that I was his mom. His words to me when I was a child, "When do I get to come see you *again*?" His familiarity with me. The oddity of feeling like I was his mother at times, even when I was only a child myself. My comfort in his presence, even when he scared me. (Isn't that what all children do to their parents?) It all started to make sense. After that realization, I started to check in with my own feelings about William. I often thought, and part of me hoped, that maybe William was waiting to be born to me in this lifetime. I thought, *Maybe, when I do get pregnant, it will be a beautiful little boy with blond hair and blue eyes.*

As I have grown older and had multiple complications with endometriosis and polycystic ovarian syndrome, my hope of becoming pregnant has been more and more challenged. In early 2018, Brian and I found out that our chances of having a child will likely depend on implants, procedures, a lot of trust in our doctors, and more money than we have stashed away. We were, and are, devastated by that news. My grief goes deeper than most can imagine because my chance to bring my friend and child back into the living world has diminished into the darkness of night that he walked into all those years ago. My hope has now become a longing, a distant wish that, one day, I will see him again and maybe ask, "Where have you been?"

If not in this lifetime, then the next.

21

A BRAKE IN THE ACTION

*It's not only moving that creates new starting points.
Sometimes all it takes is a subtle shift in perspective,
an opening of the mind, an intentional pause and reset, or
a new route to start to see new options and new possibilities.*
—Kristin Armstrong

When I see children playing, my first thought is usually of William. I welcome the reminders of him and sometimes wonder if he is orchestrating moments from the other side to make me smile. I also wonder if he isn't creating moments to give people around me a slightly new perspective.

As I've said before, Brian is a man of proof and science, a dubious believer in his own supernatural experiences. He will always second-guess the unexplainable happenings around him if there is even a chance that something could be explained by evidence. Fortunately for me, some things just can't be explained away.

On occasion, Brian and I will go on long car rides to look at the beautiful scenery around Minnesota and Wisconsin. Brian loves to drive. I love to look out the window. But he and I both know that car rides make me sleepy. My head tilts back, my mouth flops open, and I drool, snore, and talk in my sleep, but for some reason, he still takes me along for the ride.

These car rides take us to small, remote communities with cute little shops, secluded residential areas, kiddy parks, and tiny town halls. There is almost always ice cream on the trip, mostly because I whine like a three-year-old if there isn't. We watch the people who are out and about, if they show themselves. Often, residents are holed up in the local café or bar, or maybe they are just hiding from the strangers passing through town.

Oddly, I was awake for this specific trip and loved every minute of it. The roads wound gently between quaint houses with big yards. As we approached one home, I could see the spirit of a small boy playing with a big, pinkish-red, rubber ball in the front yard. His hair was dark brown and due for a trim. It fell in his eyes as he ran, squealing with glee and flailing his arms wildly, trying to catch the bouncing ball. As we approached I had the feeling that his ball was going to roll into the road in front of our car.

I played out the scenario in my head and decided not to say anything to Brian. My reasoning was twofold. First, the boy was a spirit, and getting hit by a car wouldn't hurt him. Second, and most important, Brian can't see spirits, so warning him that there was a spirit boy on the side of the road wouldn't make a difference.

I leaned my head back and watched the little boy. The ball bounced off the packed dirt in his yard, hit a tree root, and veered into the street. It came to a stop smack dab in the center of our lane. The boy plowed into the road at full speed, his arms outstretched to retrieve his ball.

Brian slammed on the brakes. With the most frantic look on his face, he turned to me and said, "What was that?" Being the supportive and lovely wife that I am, I responded with a sideways smirk and a "What?"

The car was at a dead stop. The little boy was standing in the road, ball in hand, staring up at the grill of the car. Brian pleaded with me to tell him what had just happened. He couldn't explain why he slammed on the brakes. I asked him several times to tell me why he did, and he said that he thought he'd seen something and felt like he needed to stop right away. After a few moments, he started to drive again but continued to plead with me to tell him what I saw.

I told him about the little boy and his big, pinkish-red ball. Brian fell silent for a minute and then wondered out loud whether he actually saw something or if it was just a fluke that he'd slammed on the brakes. He could not deny that he saw and felt something, but he wasn't quite ready to accept what it was.

We drove for a long time that day, his questions lingering in the air. Then a confused, "I don't know why I did that," interrupted the quiet. As the words fell from Brian's mouth, I just sat there with a smile, thinking, *Yes, you do, honey. Yes, you do.*

22

EMPTY SPACES

*As we look into the empty spaces within us,
we often find new life that we did not know was there.*

What is it about empty, noiseless spaces that makes us feel as if, at any moment, something is going to pop out and grab us?

Generally speaking, my life has never been noiseless. A constant chatter of spirits, angels, or my own voice fills the air like the scent of roses in a flower shop on Valentine's Day. When it does grow quiet, fear sets in. Quickly.

There are days when I fear my gifts are gone, months when I worry that I am losing my touch, and then all of a sudden it comes back as if returning from vacation. Perhaps my gifts were just sitting on a sandy beach and watching the sunset until the time came to catch up on all the work they missed. I am not sure if stress limits my ability to see and hear things, or if this is just a period of rest in which my body and mind can grow. No matter what it is, it is jarring and intensely uncomfortable.

Inevitably, the times when my senses are the weakest are the times when the skeptics step up to bat. I am extremely blessed in that I haven't had a lot of cynical people walk through my doors and challenge me, but a lot of unbelievers give me "the look." This expression tells me that they think I am nuts. I give them a message, and they deploy the look or, worse, deny everything that I said, only to come back months later and confess that they weren't completely honest with me and the messages were right.

I have been told that it gets easier to hear someone tell you that you're wrong about the messages that come through. I just haven't found peace with that yet. Even when I know that the messages are accurate, the thought that someone thinks I am wrong or assumes I'm losing my mind is hard to get used to. I look forward to the day when I finally feel peace around that, and peace around my fear of quiet.

Does my fear of quiet, empty spaces come from the noisy environment that is my daily life or an innate human fear that sounds fire alarms when everything seems "too quiet"? What is that? The calm before the storm?

These periods of quiet activity in my life have always cleared the way for new gifts to emerge or for the growth and acceptance of old ones. Realizing that, I have started to welcome the calm moments (after an initial stubborn search for my AWOL gifts).

It was like that the day I found out I could channel messages from the angels, ascended masters, and other higher-vibrational beings. For almost six months before this revelation, I had felt like I was just going through the motions. I was doing more massages than my schedule should have allowed, and I was exhausted. I received messages from the angels and spirits, but they were only a few sentences each rather than the lengthy verbal ramblings and images that normally came through to me during a session.

I doubted myself as a healer. I wondered whether it was time for me to stop doing the work that I loved to do. Then, as I was in a session, I received multiple images that didn't seem to make sense. They showed other worldly beings in lab coats doing experiments with petri dishes and test tubes, mathematic equations, and people speaking languages that I couldn't understand. When I got out of the session, I put pen to paper and started writing.

I don't believe I was the one writing. I wasn't thinking of

anything as I did it, and it wasn't the way I usually wrote. As the handwriting changed, so did the tone of the messages. Multiple archangels were sharing their messages through my pen. Pages later, I stopped writing, looked down, and with amazement started to read the words. I remembered nothing. Not a word on that paper had passed through my brain, and the words were not those I would normally use.

As I read the messages, I felt the exhaustion set in. Complete exhaustion. It was as if I had just run a ten-mile race but had no recollection of it. This intense channeling continued for weeks. At random times I would feel called to grab paper and pen, and I would write. I wrote out strange messages for other healers that I knew, friends, and even friends of friends. Texting became an unsettling process because I never knew what was going to come out of my fingers. Luckily, I trusted that no matter what came out, it was a message that was meant to be heard. Each message was unique, and I often did not read them if I knew they were for someone else. I just handed them over and trusted that the messages were correct. (They were.)

This new gift not only exhausted me, but also gave me a newfound trust in my abilities. I had to believe that the information that was coming forward was accurate and necessary for the specific moment in which it was written. For some reason, I trusted the gift of written messages far more than the verbal messages I normally received. It had to be the use of big words. (I didn't know what half of them meant!) Someone much smarter than I am was writing those messages.

Still, the channeled writing left me exhausted each time. I asked that the messages slow down. I couldn't keep up, and they were interrupting my daily life—I felt compelled to keep pen and paper near me so that I didn't miss an important message. I didn't want to be held captive by my own gifts, with no control over when they surfaced: I wanted to be in tune with them.

It wasn't until that point that I truly understood that I could set boundaries on what information came in. Don't get me wrong: I always knew that I had some control, and my experience with Magdalena and Alex had helped me to create boundaries. It just didn't fully sink in until that day how much control I really have. As with most lessons that I have learned, my guides stepped in to drive the point home. They channeled the following message for me through pen and paper:

> As a human being living in a human world, with human relationships, your physical body and emotional body have limitations that your energetic body can transcend. You can do all things in an energetic manner, but you must learn the balance between your body, mind and soul. Your lessons on this earth may require you to use each independent of one another, but in the end, you are human in this moment and that balance must be maintained. As a human, you are not meant to stay in any one space for too long without embracing balance.

I preach this concept to clients often, but I struggle with it too. In my life, my consistent imbalance has forced me to find balance in the only moments when I have found peace. In other words, sometimes I have to hit rock bottom in order to recognize the direction I am headed and change my course.

23

REBIRTHED AT A MEDITATION

> *Help us to be ever faithful gardeners of the spirit,*
> *who know that without darkness, nothing comes to birth,*
> *and without light, nothing flowers.*
> —May Sarton

There have been many times in my life when I have felt like I was being reborn into some other life or experience. These moments prompt me to make a significant change in my course. Only then do pieces of my past come together, until I can finally start to make out the picture of my own life puzzle. As I have grown and learned more about my gifts, the number of those moments has increased. The most intense that I have experienced so far came at a meditation.

Meditation has always been hard for me. I do not sit still well: it is my belief that every waking moment of my life should be filled to the brim in order to accomplish as much as I can while I have use of this body. During meditations, that belief often came out as involuntary wiggling of every muscle in my body, hysterical laughing fits, or deep, snoring sleep. (If I am not able to get up and move, it must be time to sleep, right?) It wasn't until I accepted the process of meditation as a meaningful experience that I started to see the impact that it could have on my life and my growth. I have replaced my laughter, sleep, and wiggling with a deep sense of peace and a plethora of out-of-body experiences. My soul leaves my body and visits other places or people, or it shows me clues about the lessons I am meant to learn in this lifetime. Most of the experiences are beautiful and peaceful, but the lessons are often convoluted and full of puzzle pieces that need to fit into the right place.

Not long ago, a colleague of mine named Nicole was leading a meditation class at our office. I was overworked and it seemed to me that supporting my team was good cover for taking some time to care for myself. We came together in a large, open vestibule with high ceilings. Natural light streamed in through the clerestory windows atop walls painted in neutral colors. The floor was made of a natural pebbled concrete, and soft music filled the air to create a safe, inviting energy. In the center of the vestibule, a large, earth-toned, circular rug lay as if it had grown there, inviting participants to find a place at its edge.

As class began that night, a sense of anxiety filled the air. There were new participants in the group who struggled, as I had, with meditation. The effort of sitting still—still a foreign concept for them—created an energy of stress and vulnerability.

Nicole asked everyone to get comfortable in their space. Many of us sank down to lie on the floor with our pillows and blankets, some roosted in chairs, and the rest sat in traditional meditation style, cross-legged on a meditation mat. I placed my two lipstick-red meditation pillows on the floor and, like a child with her blankie, stretched out entwined in a dark gray fleece blanket.

For the first ten minutes I was wide awake, completely revved up, and struggling to focus on the meditation. At minute eleven I found myself in a completely different place. I was still in my body, but my surroundings were much colder. It was as if I were lying on an operating table, waiting for surgery. I glanced around the room and felt presences standing over me, just above the crown of my head. I could feel their differences, and hear their voices. I knew they were not beings of this world without ever seeing their faces. My eyes wandered over the room and then down to my left arm. I could see the healthy, pinkish-colored skin transforming to a cold, dark, slate gray burnished with a greenish patina. My skin was dying. Parts of me were dying. I could feel death crawling up my arm, and I heard the beings say, in an almost patronizing tone, "She is almost dead on the inside anyway."

I thought about that statement. It was, sadly, true. I had felt like I was dying on the inside for quite some time. I had worked myself to the point of exhaustion and was giving way too much of my time without asking for anything in return. I felt hopeless. I felt exhausted. I felt unwanted. I felt unappreciated. I felt like I was failing. They were right, and I was angry about admitting it to myself.

I pondered this until I heard the beings say, "Let's just finish it now." As the final word came out of his mouth, I felt an icy metal blade slice across my neck like an ice skater performing at the Olympics. Smooth and calculated, very precise. It wasn't painful at first. I gasped for air and grabbed at my neck. Blood spewed from the gaping wound, and I could see it pooling around my head. I began to panic, but not because I had just been sliced ear to ear with a giant knife. I panicked because I was afraid that I was making the same gasping and gurgling noises in the meditation class. I was very aware of where my body was in the present moment as well as where my body was in my meditative state.

Blood continued to pour out from between my fingers as I tried to hold it in. It was a deep red and looked as soft as silk as it pooled on the ground. It was terrifying yet intriguingly beautiful. I could hear the gurgling in my throat and saw a trickle of blood fall from the corner of my mouth. I felt peaceful, like I knew that I had to die there in that cold place in order to be reborn for my purpose in the "real world." In this moment, in a room filled with people, I was emotionally and spiritually killing off a part of myself that I no longer needed. It was the part of me that I wouldn't allow to care for myself.

I heard Nicole say softly, "When you are ready, begin to come back into your body." I wasn't exactly sure if I had a body to come back to, so I hesitated at first. Then, as I opened my eyes, I realized that I had a terribly sore throat. I felt as if I had actually been in surgery and the doctors had just pulled out the breathing tube. The back of my tongue was swollen, my throat felt like someone had their hands around it, and I was struggling to swallow or breathe.

Worried, I reached for my neck. My eyes darted around the room and then back to my hands, checking for blood between inspecting the faces of the people around me. No one gasped, no one screamed . . . as far as I could tell, I didn't have a gaping wound in my neck. Thank goodness!

As is typical for a meditation session like this, Nicole asked if anyone wanted to share their meditation experience. I held my tongue (or, rather, my throat). I was not about to share my experience with most of the people in the room. Being looked at like I was from outer space was not in my plan for that evening.

The following day, I talked to Nicole about my experience. I knew she would understand. It was crystal clear to both of us that I was beginning a new phase of my life. My current life was quickly dying and a new life was being born out of the fleshy, decaying compost. For the next two days, my throat was like a lie detector. With every word that hid who I am or covered up my gifts, my throat became more inflamed. On the flip side, if I talked about my gifts, delivered the messages that came to me, or acknowledged the path I was traveling, the swelling subsided.

I slowly turned the pages back in my own history book to look at where I started. I couldn't remember hiding my experiences as a child, but I also couldn't remember shouting them from the rooftops. It was as if I said just enough to get by and not enough to draw attention to myself. Looking back on it, I had an extremely blessed intuitive experience growing up. Unlike a lot of intuitives and mediums, I have been surrounded by supportive people most of my life—not necessarily supportive about my gifts specifically, but about my choices in general. My parents backed me up when I wanted to try something new, they encouraged me to step out of the box of normal, and most of all, they loved me no matter what and told me so. They never called me crazy, and on most subjects, I really didn't have to fear speaking my truth to them. I was, and am, lucky to have that.

When I was at home, I never felt like I needed to act like someone other than who I was. There were periods of time when I became a muted version of myself, but I know that it wasn't because I experienced judgment at home. It was the judgment outside those walls that created fear within me about fully embracing who I was. Regardless of the external input I received, growing up with a family that supported me gave me the confidence to start speaking about my gifts, no matter how crazy I thought other people would think it sounded. Of course, it still took a while for me to start telling people outside of my small circle of friends and close family about the things that I see. It is, as some of my friends say, like coming out of the closet . . . just a different closet, the spiritual closet.

No matter what closet you are in, it is always hard to get out if there is an avalanche of clutter in front of the door. The clutter in front of mine was my own fear: fear of the reactions I would receive, fear of failing, and a tiny piece of fear that my gifts really were a sin. I compensated by lumping people into categories so I knew how to interact with them with the least amount of backlash.

Most people fell into one of three categories: those who accept, those who ignore (or ignore while hoping I will change), and those who judge. Just as it sounds, the accepters are the people who embrace me and my gifts as-is. Some share my beliefs and some do not, but I always know that in the end they will be there for me. This group has always been my parents, my sister, my friends, and the people in my healing circles. These people are my support system.

The people who ignore everything are the people I feel the need to blurt to. Like ripping off a Band-Aid, I blurt my truth as quickly as possible, hoping that my words shock them into a stupor. By the time they come out of shock, they have had a few minutes to wrap their head around it before they react. After that, some just ignore it and others silently hope my gifts are just a phase. Unfortunately, this category is where a lot of my extended family sat for years. Some have accepted pieces of my gifts, but only the pieces that conveniently fit into their belief system. The rest falls on deaf ears. Sadly, some of the people in this category have commented to me that they just want to know that I still call myself a "Christian" in public; they don't care what I do beyond that point.

The people who judge me before asking questions carry a very strong, outspoken belief that I am wrong, a sinner, or going to hell for my beliefs and gifts. Most never even get to know me: they just judge me from afar. I am fortunate that many of the people I know in this category have removed themselves from my life. On rare occasions, I still find distant family members, clients, or fellow church members who hold this belief. Some feel I need to be converted, but most have found my conversion to be a lost cause and eventually fall back into the "ignore and pray that I change" category.

While I believe that how others see us helps to keep us accountable for our morals and ethics, I also believe that at some point, we need to break free from the judgment of others. In the end, it is more important for us to rely on ourselves to choose who we are and define our beliefs and morals than to derive them from fear of what others think of us. That fear is just one part of ourselves that we must learn from and then allow to die so that we can thrive in our lives using our God-given talents.

I really came into being the day I no longer cared about what the world thought of me, only on my thoughts for changing the world.
—Suzy Kassem

24

SNOW ANGEL

*A teacher affects eternity;
he can never tell where his influence stops.*
—Henry Adams

I heard squeals of excitement as the door opened: "It's a Jenn day!" If you weren't aware, in most circles around here, *Jenn* is synonymous with *massage*. I spent the first ten years of my career traveling around the Twin Cities with my massage equipment proudly strapped to my side, and I loved every minute of it. I walked into someone's home (or office) and was welcomed by the multitude of different scents that surround them daily, the prominently displayed images of family and friends, and often the beautiful little furballs that they had adopted. On their own turf, they allowed themselves to be vulnerable when they normally wouldn't and speak freely of things that they would normally keep private. I was blessed with trust.

As the years sped along, I grew resentful of the fact that I had to turn people away. Twenty-four hours a day weren't enough for me, and my drive time was eating up the minutes on the clock. I had come to another point where rebirth and growth were inevitable. I hesitantly made the decision to settle in at a physical location closer to my home, keeping only a few of my in-home accounts active.

I also let go of all but one of my business clients. I had started working with the company in December 2006, and I felt an immediate attachment to the people there. The company's culture breeds connection, and I always felt comfortable in the environment they created. Maybe it had something to do with the fact that they allow their employees to bring their fur babies to work. Fabulous people and cute dogs: I'm in!

As the business grew older and larger, the time I spent at their location expanded as well. I was there at least every other week for eleven years, and through most of that time I remained tight lipped about my spiritual gifts. As I started sharing energetic and spiritual information with other clients, I left them in the dark. I was afraid I would scare them away with my "weird" visions and the fact that I routinely talk to dead people. Somehow, the business setting changed the playing field for me, like we were playing soccer by baseball rules. Hurling the spiritual ball at people just didn't seem to make much sense.

I laugh now as I think about my narrow vision. This company and its employees have become part of my family. I can't imagine *not* seeing them on a regular basis, and I feel silly that I ever covered up a huge part of who I am there. Sharing how they are feeling, what is going on in their lives, and how stress affectsthem are all part of the natural process of their massages. Over the years, I came to know them all fairly well. As they spill the details about their lives, I receive energetic information, messages from their guides, and messages from the angels. I used to shove much of it aside, never to be heard by their ears. I became very good at weaving bits and pieces of that information into normal conversations using the methods I had learned from Estelle years earlier. But there was so much more that I was not sharing. People who had passed on would step in to share messages, and I would ignore them. Angels would give encouragement on projects or life in general, and, again, I would ignore it. I was hiding in plain sight for absolutely no reason other than my irrational fear of judgment and fear of getting something wrong.

On January 4, 2016, that all changed. From that day on, there would be no more hiding what I heard and no more weaving the web of details into a socially acceptable package. I started sharing my gifts more fully—well, most of the time.

I was brushing my teeth in my bathroom, taking care not to get toothpaste splatter on the mirror, when Lauren, who worked at the office, casually popped into my house. She seemed very comfortable with the fact that I was in grungy workout pants and an oversized sweatshirt. I was just confused. It was just after midnight on a Monday morning, and I was expecting to see my usual slew of spirit friends. She was twenty-six years old and, as far as I knew, very much alive.

She looked at me and smiled. I know that she was trying to break the news to me in a gentle way, but my brain was short circuiting. Her smile pressed upward on her cheeks, and her eyes squinted slightly. As always, her smile was contagious. It was genuine, full of joy and kindness. Through her smile, everyone could see her light, whether they were intuitive or not!

I stared at her, shock and confusion taking over every neural pathway in my brain. It didn't make sense. My toothpaste-covered mouth was wide open like a Venus flytrap, but even with everything that was flooding in, I couldn't catch any of it.

I was still trying to wrap my head around how she was standing in my bathroom when she said, "Jenn, you have to go into the office today. Everyone needs you." To be honest, that was all she had to say. In my heart I knew that if she was standing in my house, she was no longer on this earth. If she was telling me that I needed to be there, I needed to be. I had no reason to doubt her, other than my own perception that her age disqualified her from death.

I am pretty sure that I studied her more intently than I have any other spirit. When she was alive, I never truly looked at her for longer than a quick conversation. That would have been, in terms of social norms, creepy. Now I had the chance to see how beautiful she was and how much light she carried. As humans, we buy into the social norm that tells us what interaction is supposed to be like, how long we are allowed to look at someone, and what compliments we are allowed to speak rather than just think. Looking at someone long enough to recognize their full beauty, in person, without being in a relationship with them, is seen as awkward in most situations. However, when we cross over, that story changes. Our soul wants us to be a beacon of light to others, and that she was. I finally had the opportunity to experience the unfiltered beauty of her light.

Slowly, my Venus flytrap of a brain started to catch the information that was flying around my head. Spirits don't usually step forward with messages this quickly, and I knew that she couldn't have been gone long because it had only been a week since I was at the office last. Someone would have told me. When people cross over, there is a bit of a learning curve, for us and for them. Just as we have to learn how to communicate with people on Earth and those who have passed, they have to learn to communicate with us. The older the soul, the easier this communication becomes, because they have already been through it. The opposite is true for younger souls. When souls pass on, their natural energetic vibration changes frequency, and in order to connect with people, they have to lower their vibration or find someone who can raise theirs to match. On either side of the veil, it can take an immense amount of energy to do this. I concluded that either her soul was a veteran or she was a really quick study. It was likely a little bit of both.

As I looked at her, I started to get images of the thick, murky energy that was around her heart while she was alive, and the pieces started to come together in my head. I remembered conversations that I had with her about muscle tension that I was feeling, and I flashed back to a moment months before when I told her that the energy around her heart was low. We had a quick conversation about what was going on in her life and attributed it to relationship changes. It started to occur to me that I hadn't paid full attention to the energy that was there. I wasn't listening. I knew that her physical body gave up because something happened in her heart. She would later tell me that she didn't feel any pain because her soul ascended moments before her body gave in. It was her time.

Walking with her, I went to get confirmation. As much as I didn't want to, I searched the obituaries and instantly found hers on the *Star Tribune*'s website. It read, "Lauren . . . Age 26 . . . passed away unexpectedly Thursday, Dec. 31, in Minneapolis from an aortic aneurysm." My heart sank. Part of me had hoped that it wasn't real. The sinking feeling grew worse when I allowed myself to think of the sadness and pain that were sweeping over everyone who knew her—a sadness deep enough to call Lauren to my home after midnight and ask me to take action without a request from anyone at the office.

When I first met Lauren at the office, I honestly thought that she hated getting massages from me. She was very quiet about her experience and usually didn't say much after her massages, even in the moments when I let my filter down and approached the subject of energy with her. A quick hello as she walked past me or a "How are you?" was the extent of our interaction for a long time. I thought that she was just getting a massage because everyone else at the office did. Eventually, not too long before she passed away, she decided to move to Colorado. She told me about her decision during one of her massages before she left. It was the first time that she really opened up to me.

The last time I saw her alive, she was back in town for a brief visit and I finally found out how much she liked getting massages from me. I could feel the stress in her body while I worked on her, and I told her that she needed to find someone in Colorado to work with her. Her response was, "How about I just ask Stephanie [her boss] to send you out there every other week?"

We laughed as I told her that it sounded like the perfect plan to me. She confessed that she missed massage day.

The morning after she visited me in my home, I woke up with no prompting other than hers and canceled as many of my appointments as I could that day. I was fully prepared to just show up at their office without warning, and I knew that it was the right thing to do. I didn't think about what I was going to say or how I was going to approach the "Lauren told me to come in" conversation. It was as if I forgot that I was hiding from the big bad wolf of judgment.

I made a last few phone calls to clients from a parking lot and then walked into the one session that I couldn't cancel that morning. My plan was to finish that session, go back to my office and pick up some of my equipment, and then go straight to their office. I was much calmer than I should have been for a girl who was about to drop an "I'm a medium" bomb on people; as far as they knew, I didn't know that Lauren had passed away.

As I drove back to pick up my equipment, I had to pull off the road to answer a phone call.

"Jenn, can you come into the office? Everyone needs you today." It was, Aaron, Stephanie's husband. I don't remember any explanation from him or any other discussion. I told him that I had already canceled my appointments and was on my way.

I assumed that my drive into the office would be deafeningly quiet. Completely out of character for me, I had the radio off and was listening to the wind as it detoured around the edges of my car and through the slight opening of my window. I still hadn't started grieving myself. Being able to see and talk to people who have passed away can make grieving an arduous task. I often grieve my losses incompletely. I don't always wholly accept the physical loss of people and don't move on in the same way people around me do. For those who don't understand or know about my gifts, my grieving often seems short-lived and insincere. Some may even be offended when I smile at an inopportune time during a funeral. From time to time, I forget that other people cannot see what I see.

Then Lauren jumped into my car and interrupted the sound of silence. She plunked down in the passenger seat, almost as if she had called shotgun and was racing to beat someone else to the seat. She talked while I drove. My brain reeled at the fact that she talked this much. In five minutes she spoke more words to me than she had in all the years I had been working with her. Through the forty-minute drive, she gushed about everyone in the office. My car, once filled with unclaimed grief, now glowed with so much love that the wind could no longer creep in through my window. Her light shined brighter than ever. She gloated as she said that their office was the best place to work—stressful at times, but the best.

I had misplaced the memory of Stephanie telling me that she had known Lauren since birth. As Lauren spoke, I remembered seeing the pictures of her as a teenager in Stephanie's office. Even though it was common knowledge, they kept their relationship very professional at the office, which made it easy to forget. Lauren didn't have to stay professional anymore. She now had the freedom to say whatever she wanted, and what she wanted to say made me cry.

Her eyes, too, welled up with tears as she summoned the memories of each opportunity that Stephanie had created for her. More opportunities than she knew how to give gratitude for. She confessed that all she wanted was to make Stephanie proud. Lauren explained how she was pushed to work harder than she thought she could and how she learned that mistakes happen—the way you handle them is all that matters. She repeatedly said how grateful she was and how much she loved Stephanie. She laughed as she told me that Stephanie was like a mother to her. "One of my many mothers . . . my fairy godmother."

As if she were reporting breaking news on television, Lauren broadcast, to me and the wind, how the girls at the office were like sisters to her. She smirked and commented that Elise may have been older and wiser than her, "but not by much!" She lifted her chin, glanced up to the sky, and tilted her head back like she was going to laugh, but she didn't. Then there was a long pause, and her head dropped. Her light dimmed ever so slightly as she said, "I never let them see the person that I am outside of work." She was so worried about being professional that she often stifled her own personality at work. It was the first time that I saw regret in her face. She sat quiet for a minute. I saw myself in her in that moment, often stifling who I am to remain professional.

Lauren drifted back to the present moment and continued to declare everything wonderful about her officemates, her friends, and her extended family. She talked about how her dog, Blue, used to eat everyone's stuff at the office and how she thought that Blue missed Ailla's shoes the most. She explained how Grace was always looking out for her—for everyone, really. She always knew that if something went wrong, Grace could somehow make her feel like it was taken care of. It was her nature, and it made Lauren feel safe and less anxious about making mistakes. She divulged that Aaron would ask her questions that somehow always helped to inform some big decision in her life. He would offer his input on things, and even though it wasn't always the input she wanted to hear, she knew it was his way of showing her that he cared and was trying to help. She stopped again and then added, "They were all so good to me. I hope they all know how much I love them."

By this point, my car was at risk of flooding from the inside out, my face was puffy, and I was in a full-on ugly cry. Her love for everyone in the office was like the warmth as the sun hits your skin after a long Minnesota winter or the joy that a puppy feels when its owner comes home after a long day of work, but multiplied by a hundred. My brain stumbled over itself as I tried to pull myself together. I did not know how I was going to step out of my car and into that office without sobbing . . . and she was not done making me cry yet.

The conversation shifted slightly as she spoke about her role in the office now that she had shed her physical body. She vowed to help everyone in the office when they were struggling. I have seen this in action since then. She boasted of her new role as an omnipresent force. She was filled with pride as she explained her ability to be everywhere at once, assisting others.

She described a peace in knowing that she had a much larger purpose than she had expected. As we rode in the car that day, I became a student, taking in the words that she wrote on the chalkboard of my mind. She detailed her newfound spiritual sight for me. As she scans crowds of people, she can see everyone's light. She can see their gifts as fully as she can see their struggles. Her love and dedication to her work at the office were extracted with each word spoken, and she proclaimed, "I am still going into work . . . when I feel like it!"

I also received a bit of an unexpected inquisition while we were in the car. "Why do you hesitate to use and speak of your gifts?" she asked me several times, gently. Luckily for me, I was still sobbing too hard to answer her. Like gum under a table, her question stuck with me. Brilliantly, she used that moment to segue into talking about one of her other officemates, Robert. He was allowing his own intuitive gifts to stagnate. Like me, he didn't always use the gifts that he knew were there. She alluded to being prompted to call both of us out on it. By whom, I am unsure.

For a few minutes, her tone changed and she became more serious than she had been for most of the ride. She spoke of Robert's current gifts and the ones that were about to be revealed to him. His gifts were surfacing as they silently developed, but he was pushing them away. She was here to help and wanted me to share that with him. She wanted to mentor him from the other side. "He can practice with me!" she said enthusiastically. She truly wanted to see him flourish and fully utilize his gifts. Her thought was that Stephanie had always believed in her, and because of that, she was able to accomplish things she didn't think she was capable of. She could see Robert's gifts emerging, and she knew he could do more than he thought he could. Without hesitation, I agreed to share the message with him; being a fellow healer, he was the only one in the office with whom I had started to share my gifts.

I was shocked at the amount of relief I felt when she revealed that not everyone would be ready to hear their messages yet. I hadn't allowed myself to think about how anxious I was about walking into the office with this information. Delivering messages to one person, even someone who fully understands my gifts, can be hard. Delivering messages to multiple people who have no idea what I do is like standing in front of a blind firing squad: you have no idea what will happen but fear the worst in the end. Many of them wouldn't be ready for their messages for over a year.

As we got closer to our destination, she recited a poem to me. She had written it to help everyone see that she was still here with us. After she finished, she asked me if it was corny or cheesy. I smiled and, jokingly, said, "Yes, horribly." Taking my sarcasm to heart, she agreed and asked that I forget it.

It was a beautifully written poem, perfect for the January day. The powerful images that she painted locked themselves into my memory as a clear depiction of her love.

She described the seasons we would walk through in our lifetimes and how she would be there each step of the way. She spoke of the "newly fallen snow, white and shimmering as it created mounds and snowbanks along the roadsides. Step by step she walked on top of the banks, her footprints forming beside us like a shadow on a sunny day." I pictured myself on that snowbank, following each word that she said as if it were directions on how to live my life:

We walked along the snowbanks surrounded by the feather-like snow that fell from the sky. Play, she said. Allow yourself to lie beside me and spread your own wings upon the earth. As you rise up, you will see that I was there with you, my angel wings spread in the snow on the ground as proof. I am here, I am always here, surrounding you with the protection of my snowy white feathers.

As the winter fades, I will shower you with tears of joy from the heavens. I am proud of you. I see what you have done, I see how you have healed, I see how you have accepted yourself and allowed others to love you. Play. The puddles wash away your sadness, your pain, and will forever remind you of me.

Spring will end, and summer will come. I will smile upon you, and the sun will shine. Enjoy the beaches, dip your toes in the sand, and know that the warmth you feel is my arms wrapping around you.

As the leaves change, so will you. It is time to release your grief, your fears, your anger, and know that I have been with you this whole time. Let go as the trees do: drop everything so that you can start over again. We can start fresh, without regret and without pain.

The images were so vivid as she spoke the words. I wish I hadn't joked that it was cheesy. Then maybe we both would have taken the time to remember the words more fully.

As I entered the office that day, the air was stale and grief permeated the building. Eyes were puffy, smiles were very half-hearted, and everything was quiet. I did energy work on everyone that day, and no one asked what I was doing or why I was doing it. Lauren walked from room to room, asking people to smile. Unknowingly, they would. Their energy would change as she walked in. Auras brightened again, if only temporarily. Even though I knew they could, on some level, sense her presence, it was hard for me to think I was the only one who knew for certain that she was still around.

The day of Lauren's funeral, I gave myself plenty of time to get there. I was half expecting another dissertation on the new life of Lauren while I drove there. As I was getting in my car to leave, I slipped and caught my pants on something sharp. A hole the size of my fist now graced the leg of my pants. After the cuss words flew from my mouth, I took a deep breath and got in my car. I couldn't walk into her funeral with torn pants, so I started my car and rushed toward home. This was going to add forty-five minutes to my trip, but I would still have ten minutes to spare if everything went smoothly. I took another deep breath and told myself, "Don't panic. It is fine. You will make it on time." Even with my spare ten minutes, I sped home, worried I would be late. My emotions were high, and I have a bit of a lead foot anyway, so what happened next shouldn't have surprised me.

Ten minutes from home, I saw a police car pull up behind me. Cherry-red lights were the last thing I wanted to see in my rearview mirror that day. The sound of the siren ripped through me. I was hoping my car would have magically disappeared before the officer saw that I was going eight miles an hour over the speed limit, but that was not the case.

As the officer approached my car on the shoulder, my emotions got the best of me and I started bawling. I rolled my window down, and when he asked if I knew why I got pulled over, I responded with an almost unintelligible "Yes." Tears and snot streamed down my face and I managed to get out a hysterical stream of words: "I am supposed to be on my way to a funeral for a girl that was way too young and I tore my pants so now I have to go home and now I got pulled over and I am not going to make it to the funeral on time and I am having a really bad day."

His eyes were huge, and he just kept saying, "It's okay, miss. I'm not trying to make your day worse. You just need to slow down. Okay?"

I replied, still in hysterics, "I'm going to miss the funeral, and I still have to change my pants."

Lauren popped into my passenger seat as I said it and started to laugh. I did not find it even the slightest bit amusing. The look on the officer's face, the absurd words streaming from my mouth, and the gaping hole in my pants were incredibly funny to her. "It is not important for you to be there," she assured me through her giggles.

Luckily, the police officer let me off with a warning, and I was back on my way. While I was not going to make it to the funeral, Lauren reminded me that my little detour meant that Brian could now ride with me to the celebration of life after the funeral, and I wouldn't be rushed. It was her gift to me that day.

Many months later Lauren came to me to deliver a new message. As she spoke, she seemed more distant than normal, almost anxious. It was as if she were loitering in her own memory. She approached the subject of the celebration of life after her funeral. I saw her there that night. She wore a conservative black mini-dress that sparkled as the lights hit it; her hair was down, and an ear-to-ear smile shone on her face. She floated through the room like she was a princess at a ball and everyone wanted to talk to her. She laughed as she heard the stories people were sharing.

As she described her memory to me, she shared how she loved that complete strangers were talking to each other. Most of all, she loved that people were laughing and smiling while sharing in her favorite foods and beverages. A softly spoken soliloquy fell from her lips: "It was perfect."

As people had watched the slideshow of images of her projected at the celebration of life, she had watched their reactions. Her radiant personality was being unveiled in that moment to people she had wished had seen it sooner. She no longer hid behind her professionalism, she no longer worried about how she would be seen, and she was relieved when everyone's face lit up when they saw pictures of the other Lauren. She listened as many talked about how they didn't know "that Lauren." I saw the regret on her face again; she truly wished she had shown them. She had watched as one of the gals from the office pulled out her phone to show me a picture of Katrina, another officemate who had been at the People's Choice Awards for work that night. Lauren saw the picture and, full of awe, said, "She looks beautiful!" I just smiled and watched her float off to talk to the next group of guests that walked in the room. All night, she moved from group to group, listening, laughing, and smiling because it was, as she said, perfect. She shared in all of those joyful moments at an event she knew was also filled with sadness.

She shared that she sees that sadness lingering in the people she loves. She spoke about how she wants everyone to be happy again and move forward with their lives. She still pops into my head space often, just to check in and tell me how I can help at the office or give me a message to pass along. She just wants to stay connected and show everyone that no matter what, she is still here and still cares.

Around the time I was trying to finish up this book for my first round of edits, Lauren stepped into a session and asked me if I realized the significance of her death to my own journey. I knew that her death impacted me emotionally, but until she asked, I didn't know how much it impacted my spiritual growth. I began to reflect on that day when she came to me in my home. She explained that my growth began with the choices I made that morning.

In the sweetest, kindest way possible, she asked, "What was different that day?" I truly had no idea what was different. I couldn't think of one thing that I thought was different for me. Then she blurted, "Jenn, you didn't question. You canceled your sessions, no questions asked."

She was right. For the first time, I did not question the information that I was receiving. I did not stop and mull over how it would be received if I just showed up at the office on a day that I wasn't scheduled. I didn't question what Aaron would say when I told him that I had already cleared my schedule and was on my way. I just did what I was asked to do. No questions. No worries. No judgment. No fears.

I can't say that I have kept that fearless attitude all day, every day since then, but I certainly don't hide like I used to. I know that I don't have to hide because Lauren walked me through it, just like William used to. That day, Lauren walked into my house and told me exactly what I needed to do. As she spoke now, the light bulb lit up above my head. I felt as if I needed guidance and was receiving it.

She declared, "I want you to use this in your book." I laughed to myself and thought, *You just want to be in my book!* As if she could hear my thoughts (which she probably could), she said, "Not that I want to be in your book." There was a short pause and then, with childlike innocence, she gave a half smile, tilted her head to the side, glanced upward, and admitted, "Yeeahhh, I do!"

Honestly, she deserves to be in this book. Without her, I might have never told anyone at her office about my gifts. I might have continued questioning the information as it came in (more often than I still do), and I might not have given any of her messages to the people she loved. She gave me a reason to step out of my comfort zone and just accept what I was hearing and seeing as truth. She gave me permission to be me, fully.

I never would have guessed the impact that she would have on my life, especially in terms of my spiritual gifts. In a relatively short period of time, she went from someone I thought hated my massages to a spiritual teacher I will be forever grateful for. I guess the old saying is true: "It's the unexpected that changes our lives."

25

WHEN RELIGION BECOMES YOUR BELIEF

Whether one believes in a religion or not, and whether one believes in rebirth or not, there isn't anyone who doesn't appreciate kindness and compassion.

—Dalai Lama

Many people walk through life learning from their pastors, priests, nuns, other religious figures, or even their parents. My spiritual teachers were people who had died and spoke to me from beyond the veil. One of those people was Jesus. For the entirety of my life, I have heard people talk about their religion, their God, their beliefs, and *my* sins. I was told that I was going to hell so many times that I had a choice: I could either start to believe it or let myself become numb to the words. While I had moments when I actually believed it, more often than not I knew that walking with the spirits around me gave me a more accurate picture of where I was headed. The people who believed I was going to hell didn't realize that I had daily conversations with Jesus. Just one fabulous benefit of being a medium.

No amount of "you're going to hell" talk was going to take that away from me. He walked me through many dark moments in my life, sits with me in church (now that I go), and shows up with an ear to listen when I feel like I can't do life anymore. His words are always honest, sometimes cutting, and often filled with humor. He speaks to me in a way that he knows I will hear.

Unlike the language in the Bible, his language makes sense to me.

He has taught me that we are not the judge and jury for other people. We judge our own actions while we are on this earth, and our jury is determined by the path we take. Each one of us must decide what our actions will be, and eventually, alone, we have to take responsibility for those actions when we ascend to the higher vibration that death brings.

For years, I have struggled with the false notion, placed in my head by well-meaning religious folks, that I am not following the plan that God has set out for me because I have accepted my gifts. It is the notion that my good deeds and the truth in my heart are not good enough for God, and no matter what I do, I am a sinner undeserving of a place in heaven. I still struggle with this judgment as I sit in church.

I talk to my friends about the belief systems that support religion. Many argue that the only way to eternal peace is through a specific organized religion and your physical presence in a church, synagogue, mosque, or other religious building. Many times, Jesus told me that our divinity does not come from the church that we go to; it comes from the church that is within us. That is the truth that I live by each day.

I have pondered that statement for years. One Sunday morning, as I sat in church, the message became very clear to me. The pastor spoke of Jesus teaching masses of people on the countryside, in towns, in whatever space he was in. It became clear to me that church has never been a physical location; it is a space within the self where the divine nature of our own creation reconnects to our source. Church is connection to the divine, not a building.

On my journey, I have been asked to leave churches, four, to be exact: one Lutheran, one Baptist, one Methodist, and one Evangelical. As a teenager, I was told in a Catholic church that I was not allowed to accept communion. I later found out that it was because I was an unbaptized "sinner." I tried to find a place that would accept my questions, my beliefs, and me. For a very long time I was convinced that it was never going to happen.

I never argued or questioned why I was asked to leave those churches, but I knew. All the requests came after I started to ask questions about faith, the reality of it, what happens after death, and how we know that the Bible is truth. I was told that I just "need to have faith" and accept the truth as it is in the Bible. Inevitably, I was then told, "I don't think you are a right fit for this church." On one occasion I was even told, "Well, I guess you are going to hell." I had heard that statement many times before, but never out of the mouth of a pastor. Jesus disagreed, and I walked proudly out of that church, knowing that he walked by my side, arm around my shoulders, telling me that I already knew the truth about that.

Accepting their word on faith was a problem for me because I could see what happened when people left this world and moved on. I talked to Jesus about my life and about the things that I saw. I heard contradictions in the words that religious leaders spoke. The interpretations of the Bible were immensely different from church to church, the messages skewed for what in many cases seemed like the pastors' own personal belief.

I heard from my older clients that, decades ago, portions of the Bible were removed because religious leaders felt that they were not an accurate depiction of the Holy Spirit, contradictory to the rest of the Bible, or portrayed women in leadership roles. That knowledge shook me a bit. I did and do believe that the Bible is full of truths. I just don't believe that it holds all of the truths. This new knowledge confirmed for me that there were missing pieces and that people were changing the message for their own reasons.

I was confused by this. How can you remove portions of a book that is supposed to be followed by people on their faith journey? How could we, as human beings, remove portions of Holy Scripture to suit our own agendas? Again, I consulted

Jesus. His words always remind me to walk my own journey and not that of others. He would say, "Your path differs from that of the others, as theirs do from yours. Do not judge what is not yours to judge." I struggle with that last part, as I think most people do. I feel a moral obligation to correct others when they are doing something that I consider wrong. I remind myself often, "Not yours to judge." Some days, I have to repeat this to myself over and over again as I watch people make decisions that I don't agree with.

No two journeys are the same, and trying to herd people onto a path that is not theirs only stifles their growth. Some lessons can be learned by watching others, and other lessons must be learned the hard way—our own way.

My guides explained it to me this way: "Each human being has unique purposes on this planet. Each has lessons that they must learn in order to attain their given purposes. No two people are the same, yet all people must learn the same lessons at one time or another to fulfill those purposes. These lessons must be learned in the manner in which it serves each person's capacity to learn. You are meant to learn from one another, free of judgment and wholeheartedly supporting each other. You must teach each other as graciously as your teachers have you and love freely so that you may open your heart and accept love in return. You must show compassion, gratitude, strength, and encouragement as well as a willingness to accept everyone as they are in each moment. Just as your flaws can make you weak, they can also make you strong; so too can your strengths make you weak. You must accept your uniqueness in life, for you are the only one who can truly fulfill your purpose on earth to be uniquely you."

Each day I receive more knowledge than the last, but I am human. I stop listening when I don't want to hear, when I feel like the message is too hard, or when I am too stubborn to admit that I must make a change in myself. I would love to write this book knowing that I have all the answers to my problems and have accepted everything that has been given to me with grace and ease, but that is not the case. Each day I wake up with more questions than the last. Each day, I wake up with new judgments of myself for things that I thought I worked through years ago. Each day, I struggle to find balance between who I am and who the world thinks I should be. Each day, I am human. We are all human.

As I walk into church each week, I ask myself if this is where I am supposed to be. I ask myself, "If people in this church knew all my gifts, all my quirks, all my questions, would they still accept me for who I am? Would they still allow me in small groups? Would they still smile at me and compliment the hat that I chose to wear?" I would like to think so, but my experience tells me otherwise. If I were to stand on the stage of many churches and proclaim my gifts, I would be judged and judged harshly, not by the divine, but by the very people who sat next to me and made small talk the week before.

That is the truth for many intuitive healers. There are many who would label us sinners. There are many who pray for us to change our ways and others who avoid us altogether. I would love to believe that this has changed since the four churches shunned me, but when I am honest, I know that my beliefs often threaten their very belief system. My gifts are, according to some interpretations of the Bible, sins, works of the devil, or reserved only for prophets and holy men.

This is, of course, not a universal belief, but unfortunately enough people believe it to scare gifted intuitives and psychics into hiding or, worse yet, to completely deny their own spiritual gifts. I have been lucky enough to find a core group of people willing to accept me for who I am and where I am in my own journey. I have been able to speak freely about my gifts with my friends, family, and clients without much backlash. I have been far luckier than most.

On a fairly regular basis, I hear people question their own faith.

I hear them struggle to find peace for themselves, and I wonder if everyone struggles with their own spirituality. I wonder if atheists, spiritualists, Unitarians, Christians, Jewish people, Muslims, Pagans, scientists, and everyone else all struggle with the same questions. After all, if we think about it, we are all created by the same force; we just call it something different. Most people believe that their god (or belief) is the only true god and creator of humankind. In my understanding, that means that we each believe that our creator created everyone else. Right? Wouldn't that also mean that, no matter who or what you believe in, we were all created from the same force or being? Wouldn't that mean that we are all created for purposes that work toward the same goal set by that force?

These are the questions that I have asked for years. I was prompted to ask them on my journey to find truth, and I believe that no matter how we respond, the answers bring us closer together in our individual and collective journeys. We are all the same, no matter our circumstances, our job, or where we came from. We are all on a journey to find the truth, and we can only find it when we are willing to look deeper than what society tells us is accurate and true.

26

A YEAR OF HEALING: THE NOT-SO-FINAL CHAPTER

Did I offer peace today? Did I bring a smile to someone's face? Did I say words of healing? Did I let go of my anger and resentment? Did I forgive? Did I love? These are the real questions. I must trust that the little bit of love that I sow now will bear many fruits, here in this world and the life to come.
—Henri Nouwen

Each time I sat down to write my truth, I tried to convince myself that it would be an easy process. "I'm a fabulous writer," I told myself. "There won't be any edits necessary!" spewed out of my brain as I pecked away at the keyboard. I boasted to myself, "I have finally healed enough to share my story." My spirit guides had told me that I would complete my book by my birthday in April. However, they did not tell me what year, and I hadn't thought to ask. I had the misconception that because I was called to write this book and because it was a story that I was very familiar with, it would be easy; my perceived nine-month deadline for completion would be a breeze.

Naïve hardly describes my state of mind when I finally sent off the first draft. I hadn't shown a single person before I sent it to my editor, and a few of my author friends gasped when they found out. I was so fearful of what people would think that I thought I could just skip all the anticipated judgment and move straight to bestseller status with no stress. I thought I had healed enough to complete my story. The contrast of that thought with the fear floors me.

My editor sent it back to me, coated in suggestions, questions, and red "ink." It forced me to take more time with my book . . . as well as the memories I had buried in the back of my mind in a refusal to confront them. It was in this space that I truly started to heal from the images that I carried with me. It is where I allowed myself to become vulnerable and open up to the people around me more fully. As humans, our healing work is never done.

For almost a year I have teetered back and forth between working on and turning my back on the memories written on these pages. I have sobbed as I remembered the images from my childhood, the conversations with Jesus, the judgment that I hate to face, and my own, often contradictory emotions. My healing began with the first few pages of this book but was catapulted to a new level when I was hit with a spate of events meant to heal my emotional soul wounds.

To the naked eye, the first event seemed to be an everyday example of my life. I agreed to do something fun to raise money for charity. However, the impact of it caught me completely off guard.

Sitting at a volunteer convention lunch, I played with my long hair as I listened to my friend Matt talk about shaving his head for a cancer care initiative he had started. Fingers entrenched in my hair, I verbally poked at him, "Why didn't you ask me if I would shave my head with you guys?" His laugh said it all. He didn't think I would shave off my fifteen inches of healthy brown hair. Feigning indignation, I spouted off, "You obviously don't know me at all if you think I won't do it! You raise enough for the cause, and I am there!" I had many family members, friends, and clients who had been affected by cancer, and shaving my head for a cause like this was on my bucket list! Matt didn't know, but I was all in, no matter the amount raised.

The excitement energized me as I walked out of the luncheon to assist with a seminar. Then, as I walked into the session room,

I received a message from my mom: my aunt, who had fought a long battle with cancer, had passed away. Fighting back tears, I nodded to spirit, *Message received*. Now there was no doubt that shaving my head was the right thing to do.

When the day finally came, I left work, picked up Brian, and drove the four and a half hours to Mahnomen, Minnesota, where a banquet room full of people waited. Most had no idea I would be the one shaving my head for their cause. As friends, acquaintances, and complete strangers saw that I was the surprise guest, many stood there shocked that I was actually going to shave my head. Over and over again I heard the words, "Completely? Like, all the way down to the scalp?" I answered with the same mocking laugh that Matt had fired at me when I agreed to shave my head in the first place. "Yup! All the way! It is just hair. It grows back!" Underneath that comment, though, there was a very vain little part of me that was scared of what I would look like with no hair. I wondered, *Is my head misshapen? Does my scalp break out when my skin gets irritated?* Then, brushing the thoughts aside, I focused on our cause.

Brian and my friends took turns navigating the scissors and razor around my skull. There was a brief pause to humor me with a picture of me rockin' a Mohawk—one more thing crossed off my bucket list. Matt and I stood in front of the room with our bald heads as the crowd cheered and clapped. People approached me to relay story after story of people who had passed away from cancer. I saw sadness and joy as they recounted their lives with their loved ones, and I wondered when one of those loved ones was going to come to tell me their story from the other side. Without my hair in the way, oddly, I felt more open to receiving messages from spirit. I felt as if I were no longer able to hide.

The months that followed opened my eyes further. I had in fact been hiding for my entire life. I realized just how many people were only vaguely aware of my medium life and my paranormal experiences. My new look prompted me to explore who I am in a way I had not felt comfortable doing before. What else had I been hiding from the world?

People looked up to me for doing something out of the social norm, and it gave me reason to believe that I wouldn't be judged for being different anymore. My new look had given me the freedom to be myself. I gained so much from the "loss" of that fifteen inches of hair, but it was only the first of many steps to releasing the emotional burdens I carried with me.

There was far more dead weight that I needed to release, and a deluge of healing moments was beginning. The weight of the images I had seen in Denise's basement as a child was lingering much closer to the surface than it had since I'd quarantined it twenty some years prior. I had gaps in my memory surrounding those events, and yet I intimately knew my fearfully uncomfortable feelings surrounding them. The gargoyle-like creatures—those torturous images—had been locked in a box in the back of my brain along with the conversation in which I learned who Jay was. I had buried my trauma to protect myself, and remembering the conversation with Jesus would have forced me to remember why I started asking about him in the first place. Up until this point, I hadn't been ready to relive those memories.

I was urged to look more closely at my memories and see what details I had glossed over or skipped altogether. Without hesitation, I retorted, "I can't remember anything else: this is all I remember." I hadn't thought about it, and I didn't want to think about it. I knew the source of my fear and discomfort was there, staggering around in the back of my brain like a drunk who was one beer away from a belligerent outburst.

Silence surrounded me in my meditation room as I snuggled up in my comfy chair, working diligently to edit my story. When I got to chapter 8, my stomach churned and I decided to skip over it. That belligerent drunk in the back of my mind raised his glass each of the six times I skipped that chapter. On the seventh time, he swallowed the last swig of beer and I started to read my own words. I pictured myself opening the first toilet seat, and a flood of locked-up memories broke through the dam. Tears rolled down my cheeks. Fear, curiosity, and dread all filled my body at the same time. I had opened the box, and there was no going back. I sat there, watching the movie of my life play out in front of me. I watched that creature approach me, I felt its anger toward Jay, I listened to the torturous screams, and I felt elated as I heard the gentle words of protection: "I think you have seen enough."

My body fell into a fit of sobs. For hours, I sat in my chair, staring at a knotty pine wall and sobbing. Every ounce of fear from my past, every piece of sadness that I felt for those souls being tortured, and every reason that I had hidden these memories away rose to the surface with each tear that fell. How could the tortured souls who were stuck in that space be released? Could I even help them now? Did they need my help at all? Why was I meant to see that as a child? So many questions filled my mind and then evaporated with my tears.

Then, without a moment's notice, the weight lifted. The fear was gone, and only one memory remained in the box. There were no more scary images to release, only images of a long-forgotten conversation with William and Jesus. A brief feeling of anger came over me as I remembered thinking that Jay had lied to William, and then I breathed a sigh of relief. I remembered. For so long I couldn't remember how I found out that Jay was Jesus. I tried, but I could never put my finger on the moment when I finally knew. My sobs turned to a fit of laughter. I saw the absurdity of the fact that releasing the contents of this scary box made me feel emotionally and spiritually full. I was starting to remember my truth, every piece of it.

I thought about my experiences with William and began to mourn his loss again. He had been gone for far too long. I missed my friend, and I missed the thought of having him as a child. A deep sorrow came over me, and I decided that I needed to take a break from my revisions.

Days turned into weeks, and weeks turned into months. Each week, I vowed to go back and work on the edits, but I just couldn't. It was bringing up too many emotions. I was struggling with stress in multiple areas of my life already, and adding old memories to the mix was an emotional disaster waiting to happen. The sorrow that I felt about William was exacerbated by the fact that I was still working through the lingering effects of my past-life memories. Although I wanted to let go, I was still struggling to part with the memories of Symon. I needed to release his memory so that I could move on, and as much as I hated to admit it, I knew I could not do it on my own.

As hard as I tried to stay strong and heal myself, I couldn't. My stubborn Taurus side was leading me to more stress, and when my friends invited me to attend a healing circle or a sacred fire with them, I graciously bowed out, claiming that I was too busy, had a volunteer commitment, or had to work. My excuse was always true, but I knew I could have planned ahead or made the time for myself. Even after everything I had already worked through, I still sat in fear, trying to hide that I was afraid of being seen as an inadequate healer and even more scared that my issues with fear would show everyone how broken I had become. I couldn't get my emotions sorted out, and I felt like I didn't have my life together. I didn't want to admit it, not to myself or to anyone else.

My friends wouldn't let me get away with it, though. They invited me to join them at a sacred fire at a local farm used for healing ceremonies. I knew I needed to go. I knew it would be a source of healing for me, but I also knew that going meant admitting my brokenness to a group of healers: strangers and friends alike. On the fourth invitation, I finally listened and gave in despite my fears.

As we pulled up to the farm, I had an uncertain feeling in my stomach. I knew I was going to be called into the circle for healing that night. It didn't matter how many people were there: I knew it was my turn.

I choked back tears when I verbalized my fear of holding a place in that circle. I expressed gratitude for the invitation and spoke of the call that I felt to be there on that night. I was hopeful that if I were called into the center of the circle for a healing, it would be the end of my struggle with my past-life memories.

Much of that evening swirled together like a tornado. I was indeed called into the circle. I was asked to choose those who would help me heal. I was being called on, and spirit was pushing me to ask for help. I recognized how vulnerable I felt. With my healing team by my side, I was asked to lie next to the fire on a buffalo-skin rug used for healings. The area was cleared with sage, and drumming began. A child was asked to speak into my ear, and her words still hold space in my mind. Her face next to mine, her breath soft on my cheek, I heard her words: "It's okay to cry. It's okay to cry." My mind raced. *Is it okay to cry? I need to be strong! I cannot let these people see me cry!* She continued, "It's okay to cry. It's okay to cry." The drumming got louder, and I thought my eardrums were going to burst.

My emotions seeped out of my body and onto the rug. Tears dripped from my face, and dampness pooled in my ears. I could feel the weight of my emotions being lifted. Symon's face flashed before me and was immediately released, but something else was waiting to be released as well. I could feel how close I was to letting go of this mysterious thing when I saw an image of William. I felt the flow of emotions stop. Magdalena touched my arm as if to reassure me it was okay to let go, but she felt, as I did, that I had just stuffed something back into that old memory box and closed the lid.

I lay there, surrounded by healers, wondering what I had just stuffed away. With every breath I tried unsuccessfully to reopen that box. There were no more tears. My breathing had grown calm, and my mind was blank. I felt like I had gone in for an oil change and drained the reservoir, only to drive off before adding the new oil. In that moment, I chose to ignore the knowledge that something else needed to be released and pretend that I had been healed. At the end of the night, I left feeling as if I had accomplished something, but I knew there was more work to follow.

Three years had passed since I'd last spoken to William, and seeing his face during that healing drew attention to the hole in my heart. As I drove home, I thought of him. I wondered where he was, who he was helping, and if I would ever get to see him again. I wondered if he still thought of me. He was the only thing I could think of, and the rest of my body felt empty, yet peaceful.

I drove in silence to the store the next morning. It was a beautiful, brisk day. The fall air was getting cooler in anticipation of winter, and as I approached a stop sign, I felt that I was not alone in my car. A quick glance at my passenger seat revealed a teenage boy. His blond hair had darkened slightly, but I knew those eyes. Stopping the car in the middle of the road, twenty feet from the stop sign, I stared at him.

"William?" My voice hung in the air. I couldn't believe my eyes. He had grown up. How had he grown up? He was a very handsome teenager. With a smile and a half laugh, I joked, "You have grown up!" He looked at me with gentleness and smiled.

Then his smile evened out, and in a loving, quiet, but serious voice, he said, "I don't need you anymore." The air left my body. His eyes turned downward. He knew I needed to move on. I knew it too.

My eyes welled with tears, and my voice became meek. "But, I . . . I . . . need you . . . "

He was already gone. I sat parked in the middle of the road for ten minutes as I stared at the passenger seat of my car. He wasn't coming back. The love in his voice was comforting, but seeing him grown up and healthy was exactly what I needed. He had moved on to assist others, and he was okay. I opened up the box in the back of my mind and emptied out the contents. Another weight had been lifted, and the healing that I had begun the night before was now complete.

When I got home, I opened my laptop and began to write again. I started to fill in the gaps that I had skipped in my story. I started to acknowledge the pieces of myself, the memories and the fear, that I thought were too ugly to accept. I cried without feeling uncomfortable. The healing continued, but it was still not complete.

As the weeks flew by, I continued to work on accepting my past. As memories entered, I would acknowledge them, look for the lesson in them, and allow them to be released. During this process, my spirit guides prompted me to attend a sacred ceremony with two of my spiritual teachers. I didn't know what I was getting into but was ecstatic when they accepted my offer of help to set up the ceremony space.

I arrived at the camp where we would be holding the ceremony and was greeted by an unexpected spirit. Lauren stood in the snow outside the lodge.

"Hi!" she cheerfully hollered as she walked away down one of the trails.

Why in the world is Lauren here? I thought. Then I shook off my confusion and walked into the lodge, where I was greeted with smiling faces and warm hugs.

My task for the day was to collect items from nature to create connection and beauty within our space. As I received my instructions from my teachers, my guides pushed me out the door into the newly fallen snow. Their energy was playful as they said, "Make a snow angel!" I laughed and plopped myself down on the ground just outside our lodge. Joy filled my heart.

Over the course of the weekend we shared the deepest parts of our souls with the other participants as we talked about stepping into our own power. Words and tears fell freely as we spoke in circle. Anger, joy, sadness, fear: every emotion you could think of entered that space to be acknowledged. Beautiful connections formed, and each person became an unconditional support for everyone else.

Together, we hiked the trails in silence. We each listened to our internal dialogue and the movement of emotions and energy that had called us to this space for healing. It invited us to reconnect with ourselves while surrounded by the support of others. Then I looked up, and in front of me were the remains of a painful yet beautiful memory from my childhood. I stood in the middle of the trail looking upon a pavilion. In disbelief, I turned to see a familiar patch of trees with a clearing in the middle. A stutter formed in my breath as I tried to inhale. Silent tears began to fall onto the now-sacred ground.

I walked into the clearing and sat on a log, remembering the words of three young girls: "My mom says that people who don't go to church are going to hell." "You are going to hell!" I had been called to this place, the camp of my childhood, to relive the moment when I claimed my power and stood up for my gifts for the very first time. I felt my brain explode. The tears continued as I rose and walked the path to meet everyone on the bluff. We sang to honor our ancestors and the spirits who surrounded us in that space. Above us, a dozen eagles circled. Eagles do not typically flock, so this gesture from spirit was taken in with awe by everyone other than me. I was so lost in my tears and my memory that I sang the words of the song and saw the birds above us with no sense of what was happening.

Later that evening, three of my friends and I sat around the fireplace in our lodge. The others had all gone to bed, so we stifled our giggles as we shared stories from our lives and the happenings of the day. I started to share my story from the walk and my childhood at that camp. I told them about Jesus and my walk with him. My friend Mark's jaw dropped. He stood with a look of sheer determination on his face and ran toward his bedroom.

"I have something that I think is for you," he yelled back to me. The rest of us just looked at each other.

When he returned he clasped my hand between his hands and gently placed something in it.

"I found this on the walk today," he said. Slowly he pulled his hands away and with eyes intently focused on me, nodded for me to look. I opened my hand to see a yellow neon plastic cross on a string decorated with multiple shades of pink, purple, yellow, and blue.

We all looked at him, and I asked, "Where did you find this?" He described a location along the trail, near the clearing in the woods where I had broken down earlier in the day.

"It was strange. I was walking along and noticed something pink peeking up from the ground. I'm not sure why I felt like I needed to go check it out. . . . Well, now I know!" He smirked and shrugged his shoulders, then continued, "I grabbed for it, and it was like it grew out of the ground. It just popped out . . . it was buried."

I looked at the cross in my hand and asked, "So you came back here and washed it off?"

He let out a slightly nasal chuckle. "It came out of the ground *clean*."

I grinned as I put the necklace on. "Well then, there's that."

The day following my departure from our ceremony, I was scheduled to go into the office where Lauren had worked. Conversation carried on as normal, and Aaron asked what I had done that weekend. When I told him where I had gone, he lifted his head from the massage chair face cradle and said, "That was Lauren's camp. They just built a bench there in her honor last weekend."

I was flabbergasted. "What? What do you mean, 'her camp'?"

In an almost unbelievable twist of fate, I learned that she had been a counselor at that camp. The camp where I had first accepted myself was one of the favorite places of the woman who helped me to stop questioning my gifts and begin to trust again. As I started to think about the events of the weekend, my mind wandered to my guides urging me to make a snow angel outside our lodge. Then I understood why she was there and why I was there as well.

27

WE ARE NEVER ALONE

We are never alone on this earth, but sometimes the company we keep can make it feel that way.

My vulnerability to the truth about my life played a big role in my writing. I found myself trying to censor the truth as it came from my fingertips, lessening my gifts to normalize them. I feared that I was going to lose friends, business, and family if I continued. However, this book created a timeline for me to see the progression of my gifts on the fear spectrum. I had lived in my own fear for so long that I no longer perceived fear in the same way. My misunderstanding of the spirits around me created an environment in which I often confused discomfort with fear and fear with terror. Continuing to learn about my gifts has helped me to see the spirits for who they are and what they are trying to relay to me. My fears and discomfort have, mostly, been eradicated. Reality is everything in the moment, and if that moment is fraught with fear and discomfort, it is easy to miss the lesson in it.

I have spent nights worrying about offending the world with my belief system and experiences, and yet I remain hopeful. It is my hope that everyone who reads this book can accept that we are all on this earth to give of our own gifts with a passion that can only be matched by another human being expressing their unique gift just as fully.

It is my hope that everyone who has suffered a life of hiding their spiritual gifts can finally find their voice and allow themselves to follow their calling. To stop allowing themselves to suffer, and to find the meaning behind their own gifts.

Friedrich Nietzsche said that "To live is to suffer, to survive is to find some meaning in the suffering." I find that most of our suffering comes from our own fears and what they create when we allow them to grow out of proportion to the reality around us. While my gifts did not bring much physical suffering to my life, the emotional turmoil I experienced was a form of suffering that came out of a belief that we must all fit into a box designed by a society that is run by the fear of judgment.

Looking around, I see that belief in other people. No matter who we are, we are all bound together in this fear-based society. We carry with us the fear of wearing the wrong outfit, making a mistake, laughing too loud, crying in public, admitting our inner beliefs, saying the wrong thing, and so on. Many of us are conditioned by our culture to live in fear of being different. It is a sad thought, especially when individual gifts are planted in each of us to set us apart from one another. No two people's gifts and abilities are exactly the same, and sometimes we don't recognize our own gifts until they change someone else's life.

Today and every day going forward, I am making the commitment to step out and live my medium life in hopes of inspiring others to do the same. I may only help one person make change in their life—maybe ten, maybe even thousands—but for now, I am only aiming for one. One person who will inspire one more, who will inspire one more, who will inspire one more, who can, together, create a large change in our medium world.

SPIRITUAL TERMINOLOGY

angel: A high-vibratory being that acts as a messenger for the greater good. They are messengers from God/Creator/Source/Universal Energy. Angels have not lived in human physical form on this earth.

ascended master: A spiritually enlightened being that has lived in physical form and ascended to a higher level of consciousness by learning all the lessons necessary to ascend to a state that allows them to reconnect with source. His/her purpose is to guide all beings to take action for the higher good. Examples of ascended masters are Jesus, Buddha, Mother Mary, Melchizedek, Archangel Michael, Metatron, Kwan Yin, and Lady Nada.

astral travel: An intentional journey the soul takes when it leaves the body it is bound to while remaining connected via an energetic cord, often during sleep or meditation. Also known as an out-of-body experience (OBE) or astral projection.

clairaudience: The gift of psychic hearing. People with this gift hear clear messages from spirit and/or sounds that are not audible to the human ear.

clairolfaction: Also known as clairalience, clairessence, or clairsmesis. This is the ability to smell energy in the surrounding environment. This can come in the form of a scent message or a smell that gives clues to what the message is related to. For example, smelling roses could indicate the name Rose, a flower, or a specific cologne associated with a messenger.

clairsentience: The gift of being able to clearly feel changes in the energy patterns in the surrounding environment. This can be past, present, or future energies; physical or emotional changes in a person's body; and/or energies in specific buildings or on land. Often explained as a "knowing" or a gut feeling.

clairvoyance: The gift of clear vision. People with this gift receive images, pictures, or symbols, usually within the mind's eye or third eye.

darkness: A person, thing, idea, action, or energy that is formed by ego or sourced from somewhere other than divine energy.

demon: Also referred to as fallen angels. A low-vibratory being, perceived negative entity, or evil spirit. These beings try to encourage poor decisions and create chaos and destruction to lead people away from the light and all that is good.

divining/divination tool: A specific tool or group of tools used to communicate with spiritual beings or energies. Some examples of divination tools are pendulums, Ouija boards, tarot or oracle cards, tea leaves, and dowsing rods.

empath: A person who is extremely sensitive to the energies of other people, often to a point where they have a hard time distinguishing between their own emotions and the emotions of others.

entity: Spirits that are earthbound (ghosts), lower-vibrational energy beings, or beings from other dimensions.

ghost: An unintelligent projection of energies that are stagnant in a space. They cannot answer specific questions and continually repeat movements, scenes, or phrases. They are like a movie stuck on repeat.

God: Our divine source, the energy that protects us and feeds our souls, and that which we are created from.

healing circle: A gathering of individuals who come together to heal pieces of their body, mind, soul, or spirit in an environment prepared with sacred energy and the intention of healing.

intuition: An innate "gut sense" used to feel if something is accurate, a good fit, or correct. It is a calm assurance that something is or is not true, right, or accurate. It is said to be the "God sense" or the unemotional truth from God.

intuitive: A person who uses their intuition to find the truest answers for themselves and others. Often used interchangeably with the term **psychic**.

light: A person, thing, idea, action, or energy that is sourced from God's energy or divine wisdom.

light being: Any being that is of the light, striving to achieve what is best for the higher good.

low-vibrational energy: An energy that is perceived to be negative by human emotion or experience. This is often energy created by ego but can also be energy from other dark sources.

medium: A psychic with the specific ability to communicate with people who are no longer living.

psychic: A person with senses outside the normal range of perception. This could include the gifts of clairsentience, clairolfaction, clairaudience, clairvoyance, channeling, and more.

sacred fire: A large fire used to honor the spirits of the ancestors who passed before us and to help release stagnant energies carried by those in attendance.

sage: A sacred herb used to smudge, or clear a space or person of energies that are no longer of use for the higher good or purpose.

shadow: The ego aspects of self: human emotions and human reactions that do not serve our higher good.

smudging: A method of using herbs, resins, or incense to clear energy that is stagnant in a space or on a person. Used in many traditions for clearing the energy before a sacred ceremony.

spirit: (1) A person who has passed away and crossed over into the light. They can make decisions, hold conversations, and oftentimes can move physical items to get their point across. (2) The character or personality housed in a soul.

spirit guide: A high-vibratory being that has lived in human physical form on this earth and acts as a messenger for the greater good of an individual's learning on the earth plane. Divinely chosen for each individual to assist in the learning that is meant to be done while on the earth plane. Oftentimes their messages are confused with the voice of the human conscience. Often referred to as **guides.**

soul: The energy that gives life to the body and mind. The soul houses the spirit of a person.

HEALING & PSYCHIC DEVELOPMENT RESOURCES

There are many paths on the psychic development journey. While we hope your journey is filled with grace and ease, there are usually bumps along the road. If you need assistance moving forward, reach out. There is always someone who has been there and can assist you.

National Suicide Prevention Lifeline
1-800-278-8255

No Knots Professional Massage & Bodywork, Inc.
651-768-7102
www.noknotsmassage.com
Wellness and healing center, metaphysical products, educational workshops, and classes.

Jennifer Bierma
Author, Psychic & Healer
www.jenniferbierma.com

ACKNOWLEDGMENTS & GRATITUDE

I want to thank all the amazing people who have supported me in my life and continue to support me on my journey. There are too many to list in this section, but there are a few who were instrumental in the creation of this specific book.

To my parents and my sister, who gave me the permission that I thought I needed to be me and accepted me as the me that I am for my entire life. To Gramma, for cheering me on while you were here and for cheering even louder now that you have graduated from this plane of existence. To Brian, for loving me more than I knew anyone could in this lifetime and supporting me fully even when my life is a bit over the top or just unbelievable. To my friend Sarah, for always standing by me even when the other kids thought I was weird (and even when you thought I was weird). To my amazing healer friends, for teaching me, believing in me, allowing me to be raw and honest, and lifting me up when I thought I was falling. To the women in my writers group who pushed me to keep going and challenged me to create the book that I knew was in me. To Jesus, for wrapping your arm around my shoulder, offering an honest opinion, and helping me through my darkest times with humor and grace. To the spirits, angels, ascended masters, and other higher-vibrational beings who came before us, for your willingness to trust me with your words and also take me under your wings. To William, for walking by me for years and being my rock. To Lauren, for becoming the greatest spiritual teacher that I could ever have asked for. To those who surrounded Lauren on this earth, for allowing me to write her story within mine and for allowing my gifts to emerge without passing judgment. To Charlene and Estelle, for keeping me in line even after you left this world. And, finally, to the pastors, other religious leaders and naysayers who did not accept me into your fold: without you, I would not have learned my lessons and might have become someone that I am not.

To everyone who supported me in my journey (knowingly or unknowingly), I am eternally grateful. I am sending love and hugs to you all in this moment and forever going forward. Thank you for helping to shape me into who I am today.

www.ingramcontent.com/pod-product-compliance
Lightning Source LLC
Chambersburg PA
CBHW030442090526
44586CB00044B/574